HUMAN RIGHTS in Focus

Human Rights in Focus: The LGBT Community

Damon Karson

ReferencePoint Press®

San Diego, CA

About the Author

Damon Karson was born in San Diego and attended college at the University of California–Davis. He has enjoyed reading and writing from a young age. Outside of work, you can find him sailing, on the rugby field, or avoiding the gym.

Printed in the United States

For more information, contact:
ReferencePoint Press, Inc.
PO Box 27779
San Diego, CA 92198
www. ReferencePointPress.com

Name: Karson, Damon, author.
Title: Human Rights in Focus: The LGBT Community/by Damon Karson.
Description: San Diego, CA: ReferencePoint Press, Inc., 2018. | Series: Human Rights in Focus | Includes bibliographical references and index. |
Audience: Grade 9 to 12.
Identifiers: LCCN 2017019490 (print)| ISBN 9781682822319 (hardback) | ISBN 9781682822326 (eBook)
Subjects: LCSH: LGBT community—United States—Juvenile literature.

A Pervasive Pattern of Violence

In June 2016 Omar Mateen opened fire with a semiautomatic rifle on unarmed civilians at a nightclub called Pulse—a well-known lesbian, gay, bisexual, or transgender (LGBT) hot spot in Orlando, Florida. As Mateen stormed through the club killing everyone in his path, chaos ensued. Terrified club goers stampeded out the back door or barricaded themselves in restrooms. Others played dead. When the ordeal was over, forty-nine people had been killed, and dozens more were wounded. Mateen's rampage marked not only the deadliest act of terror in the United States since September 11, 2001, but also the largest mass shooting in US history. Another tragic and noteworthy fact about the shooting was that the majority of victims identified as LGBT.

In the days and weeks following the tragedy, the LGBT community came together and received a groundswell of support from many sectors of society. President Barack Obama showed his solidarity when he said:

> This is an especially heartbreaking day for all our friends—and fellow Americans—who are lesbian, gay, bisexual or transgender. The shooter targeted a nightclub where people came together to be with friends, to dance and to sing, and to live. The place where they were attacked is more than a nightclub—it is a place of solidarity and empowerment where people have come together to raise awareness, to speak their minds, and to advocate for their civil rights.[1]

Obama had highlighted a sobering reality: that despite progress securing rights, the LGBT community continues to be victimized by hate-fueled violence and discrimination.

Widespread Persecution

Tragedies like the Pulse shooting have garnered global attention to the many ways the LGBT community continues to be persecuted. According to a 2015 report by the United Nations (UN), many of the legal rights gained by the LGBT community related to marriage equality, employment, housing, and health care have been dramatically overshadowed by a pervasive pattern of violence against the community. Around the globe, LGBT individuals continue to be assaulted, bullied, harassed, and even killed because of their sexual orientation or gender identity. UN human rights chief Zeid Ra'ad Al Hussein highlights the extreme viciousness of these attacks: "Violence motivated by homophobia and transphobia is

A memorial is shown outside the Pulse nightclub in Orlando, Florida. In 2016, a gunman opened fire with a semiautomatic rifle in the nightclub killing forty-nine people. The club was a well-known LGBT hotspot.

often particularly brutal, and in some instances characterized by levels of cruelty exceeding that of other hate crimes."[2]

During the UN's 2012 Human Rights Council meeting, then secretary-general Ban Ki-moon called for all countries to fight against these acts of injustice:

> To those who are lesbian, gay, bisexual or transgender, let me say: You are not alone. Your struggle for an end to violence and discrimination is a shared struggle. Any attack on you is an attack on the universal values of the United Nations I have sworn to defend and uphold. Today, I stand with you, and I call upon all countries and people to stand with you, too.[3]

Despite Ban's call to action to protect LGBT communities, LGBT rights are not squarely recognized under the documents that legally protect human rights. The UN's Universal Declaration of Human Rights states, "Everyone is entitled to all the rights and freedoms set forth in this declaration, without distinction of any kind."[4] Nevertheless, in many UN member nations that have pledged to uphold the human rights of their citizens, violence, harassment, and discrimination against LGBT individuals continues largely unimpeded. In many places, for example, same-sex relations remain illegal and even punishable, which many believe creates a climate of fear and intolerance in relation to the LGBT community.

> "Violence motivated by homophobia and transphobia is often particularly brutal, and in some instances characterized by levels of cruelty exceeding that of other hate crimes."[2]
>
> —UN human rights chief Zeid Ra'ad Al Hussein

Other leaders have reaffirmed the sentiments of the UN, asserting that the ultimate goal of human rights campaigns is to create a more accepting, tolerant society so that the next generation of LGBT youth can thrive without the weight of societal prejudice and the threat of violence hanging over their heads. While the struggle for acceptance has hit numerous roadblocks, incidents like the Pulse nightclub shooting and other acts of violence serve as a reminder that some of the issues affecting LGBT individuals pose a clear and present danger to the health, livelihood, and well-being of this small but increasingly visible minority.

A Global Overview of LGBT Human Rights

The terms *lesbian*, *gay*, *bisexual*, and *transgender* describe a person's sexual orientation or gender identity. Sexual orientation refers to romantic or sexual attraction to men, women, or both sexes. Gender identity refers to the internal feeling people have that they are male or female, regardless of their biological sex, which is based on chromosomes and sexual anatomy. Transgender people, for example, describe their gender identity as different from what appears on their birth certificate. Many describe feeling like a woman trapped in a man's body or vice versa. As one transgender woman describes it: "I knew from age four on that something was wrong with me being a guy, and I spent most of my life avoiding the issue. I hid out in textbooks, pulp fiction, and drugs and alcohol. I buried my head in the sands of television, college, a lot of lovers, and three marriages."[5] She describes finding happiness once she accepted herself as a female living in a man's body.

The abbreviation *LGBT* came into use in the 1990s. It replaced the word *gay*, a blanket term that became common in the mid-1980s to describe a variety of nonheterosexual people. According to the Williams Institute, a think tank at the University of California–Los Angeles School of Law, roughly 8 million people identify as lesbian, gay, or bisexual in the United States. Another seven hundred thousand identify as transgender. These individuals have a long history of advocating for their rights, and many LGBT rights organizations operate across the nation and the world today.

A Brief History of LGBT Rights in the United States

While homosexuality has existed since even before the advent of modern civilization, the vast majority of LGBT rights have developed primarily in the past century, especially in the United States.

The first American group formed to fight on behalf of gay rights—and LGBT rights in general—was founded in Chicago in 1924. Called the Society for Human Rights, the group's founder, Henry Gerber, wrote that he wished to promote and protect the interests of people with different sexual orientations.

At the time, most states outlawed sexual acts between persons of the same gender. In addition, many religious institutions and other conservative groups regarded homosexuals as perverts and pedophiles, which contributed to widespread prejudice and discrimination. As Gerber said, "I had always bitterly felt the injustice with which my own American society accused the homosexual of 'immoral acts.'"[6] Although the group found few supporters and fizzled out after a couple of months, historians credit the Society for Human Rights as the catalyst for modern LGBT rights reforms in the United States.

> "I had always bitterly felt the injustice with which my own American society accused the homosexual of 'immoral acts.'"[6]
>
> —Henry Gerber, founder of the Society for Human Rights

The outlook for LGBT rights remained bleak for the next several decades. In the 1940s and early 1950s, for example, most psychologists and psychiatrists considered homosexuality a form of mental illness. In 1952 the American Psychiatric Association labeled homosexuality a "sociopathic personality disturbance"[7] that required extensive counseling, diagnostic examinations, and even conversion therapy, a type of so-called treatment that promised to make a gay person straight (heterosexual). That a reputable scientific organization had categorized the homosexual community as sociopathic and mentally unstable had a major trickle-down effect and continued to fuel fear, aversion, and intolerance.

To counter these negative attitudes, the Mattachine Society formed in 1950 to organize and advocate for homosexual rights. The group's mission was to "eliminate discrimination, derision, prejudice and bigotry"[8] against homosexuals and assimilate them into mainstream society. In the same vein, the Daughters of Bilitis was founded five years later to combat discrimination faced by lesbians. The organization even created the first lesbian publication, called the *Ladder*, which was published nationally until 1970. These groups started the push for more widespread tolerance of homosexuals.

Pictured are Harry Hay (left) and his partner in 2002. In 1950 Hay founded the secret network of support groups for gays known as the Mattachine Society.

The tide of public sentiment began to warm toward the concept of LGBT rights. In 1956 American psychologist Evelyn Hooker conducted an experiment that compared the mental health of homosexual men to heterosexual men. To many people's surprise, Hooker reported no discernible differences between the groups. This groundbreaking study was one of the first major pieces of scientific evidence demonstrating that homosexuality was not a sociopathic condition or mental disorder.

The Stonewall Riots

Another pivotal event in the fight for LGBT rights in the United States unfolded in 1969 at a small, nondescript bar called the Stonewall Inn, located in New York City. Although the inn was little

The Stonewall Riots and the Birth of Gay Pride

Many LGBT activists consider the June 1969 Stonewall riots as the birth of the modern gay pride movement. To commemorate the uprising, which sparked the genesis of events that celebrate LGBT culture, the month of June was designated as LGBT Pride Month. Today LGBT pride events are held around the world every June. Gay rights activist Andrew Belonsky describes Stonewall's far-reaching impact:

> The Stonewall Rebels may not have known at 1:20 am on June 28, 1969, but they were about to make history. Their actions spurred the international gay rights movement, resulting in countless cultural, legal, political, and social evolutions, including the decriminalization of homosexuality in dozens of nations. They also provided the nearly religious foundations for the greatest of gay traditions: Gay Pride.
>
> In the thirty-eight years since gays, lesbians and drag queens first lashed back at police, forty-eight countries on every inhabitable continent have held commemorative gay pride celebrations, including Turkey, Sri Lanka and Peru.

Andrew Belonsky, "Picking Apart the Origin of Pride," *Queerty*, June 18, 2007. www.queerty.com.

more than a run-down building with no running water, no liquor license, and spotty electricity, it became an extremely popular spot where homosexuals, bisexuals, and transvestites (men who enjoy dressing in women's clothing) could gather in a safe environment. However, this seemingly safe haven was not entirely free from harassment. Police officers frequently raided Stonewall, seized alcohol, and cleared partygoers from the area.

On June 28 tensions mounted. During a routine raid, police officers became particularly abrasive while handling the large crowd. Bar patrons were handcuffed, thrown onto concrete sidewalks, and beaten by police. Just after 3:00 a.m., members of the local gay community and other sympathizers turned on the police, violently throwing beer bottles and other objects. Police turned a fire hose on the angry crowds to no avail. The officers were forced to retreat from the angry mob; many took shelter inside the club and waited for police reinforcements to arrive. Protests around the streets of New York lasted for six days. By the end of the riots, several people were injured, and the Stonewall building itself had been completely destroyed.

The Stonewall riots represented a breaking point for a community that felt disrespected. One participant describes the emotionally charged evening:

> We all had a collective feeling like we'd had enough. . . . Everyone in the crowd felt that we were never going to go back. It was like the last straw. It was time to reclaim something that had always been taken from us. . . . It was total outrage, anger, sorrow, everything combined, and everything just kind of ran its course. . . . The bottom line was, we weren't going to go away. And we didn't.[9]

The Era of Gay Pride

Many consider the Stonewall riots to be the first major protest on behalf of LGBT rights. In the weeks and months that followed, gay rights groups gained momentum. LGBT people organized in support of their human rights, demanding full acceptance in society. Demonstrations around the country drew large crowds. Most importantly, groups like the Gay Liberation Front formed. In contrast to the more obscurely named Mattachine Society and Daughters of Bilitis, the Gay Liberation Front was the first group that unapologetically used the word *gay* in its name. It represented a bold new radicalism in what became known as the gay rights movement. By the early 1970s gay rights groups had formed in almost every major city in the country.

Activists also started to brazenly protest the classification of homosexuality as a form of mental illness. In line with changing social norms and pressure from LGBT advocates, the American Psychiatric Association removed homosexuality from its list of mental disorders in 1973. The American Psychological Association followed two years later. Today, in its booklet *Sexual Orientation and Homosexuality*, the American Psychological Association states:

> Both heterosexual behavior and homosexual behavior are normal aspects of human sexuality. Both have been documented in many different cultures and historical eras. Despite the persistence of stereotypes that portray lesbian,

gay, and bisexual people as disturbed, several decades of mental health research and clinical experience have led all mainstream medical and mental health organizations in this country to conclude that these orientations represent normal forms of human experience.[10]

The growing optimism engendered by these events was evident when more than seventy-five thousand supporters rallied for the passage of civil rights legislation during the National March on Washington for Lesbian and Gay Rights in 1979. The rally, which included gay men, lesbians, bisexuals, transgender people, and their straight allies, thrust the gay rights movement into the national spotlight.

As LGBT individuals became more visible in the community, many embraced what is now known as gay pride, or the idea that

Members of the Gay Liberation Front, some in drag, are arrested during a protest in London in 1971. The Gay Liberation Front represented a bold new radicalism in the growing gay rights movement.

diverse sexuality should be celebrated. Today citizens throughout the world gather to celebrate the LGBT community with festivals, parades, and other happy events. An LGBT woman explains why these events, which typically take place in June, are so empowering to members of her community: "The first time I attended a Pride Parade after coming out was a deeply meaningful experience for me. Walking in the parade wasn't just about having fun; it was a declaration of personal self-acceptance. It was a declaration that I really was a part of the LGBT community and I didn't want to hide it anymore."[11]

> "Both heterosexual behavior and homosexual behavior are normal aspects of human sexuality."[10]
>
> —The American Psychological Association

LGBT Rights Today

The twenty-first century has ushered in a series of LGBT rights victories, primarily in the United States and other Western countries. In the United States, for example, same-sex marriage was made legal by the landmark Supreme Court case *Obergefell v. Hodges* on June 26, 2015. This ruling established the right to marry for all persons in the United States and its territories. It was a hard-fought victory for those who believe that homosexual couples deserve the same marriage rights as heterosexual ones. In the majority opinion, Justice Anthony Kennedy wrote:

> It would misunderstand these men and women to say they disrespect the idea of marriage. Their plea is that they do respect it, respect it so deeply that they seek to find its fulfillment for themselves. Their hope is not to be condemned to live in loneliness, excluded from one of civilization's oldest institutions. They ask for equal dignity in the eyes of the law. The Constitution grants them that right.[12]

Another important human rights victory for the LGBT community involved the repeal of a policy known as Don't Ask, Don't Tell. This policy, which was instituted in 1994 by then-president Bill Clinton, had originally served as a compromise to the previous outright LGBT military ban by allowing closeted LGBT people to serve, as long as they kept their sexuality private. The policy claimed that the presence of gays and lesbians in the armed forces would "create an unacceptable risk to the high standards of morale, good order and discipline, and unit cohesion that are the essence of military capability."[13]

In 2010 the military conducted a survey asking service members whether they supported the policy. The findings, issued the same year, stated that most service members believed that overturning Don't Ask, Don't Tell would not thwart their ability to conduct military missions. After a series of debates, Congress voted to overturn the policy. As a result, today gays and lesbians are allowed to openly serve their country.

International Gains

Other countries have also made massive strides in securing LGBT rights. Around the world, for example, polls show increasing support for marriage equality. In 2001 Netherlands became the first country to legalize same-sex marriage. Today over thirty countries—including France, Mexico, South Africa, Spain, Sweden, and the United Kingdom—have followed suit and introduced legal recognition of same-sex marriage.

In addition, many countries have pro-LGBT policies that go far beyond marriage equality. For example, an equal rights act enacted in Netherlands in 1993 bans discrimination based on sexual orientation in housing and employment. Since then, according to the World Economic Forum, more than sixty countries—including Canada, Mexico, Norway, Sweden, and Uruguay—have enacted similar laws that ban these types of discrimination. Argentina has a particularly vibrant LGBT rights record; the country became the first to allow people to legally change their gender without requiring a court or physician to approve the change, as is standard practice in many countries. According to a 2015 report by the International Lesbian, Gay, Bisexual, Trans and Intersex Association (ILGA), some countries, like the United Kingdom and Belgium, have granted over 80 percent of the rights legally afforded to heterosexuals to their LGBT citizens.

Inequality Remains

Despite this changing landscape, human rights advocates contend that the LGBT community is far from achieving full equal-

A protester in New York marks the one-year anniversary of the public execution in Iran of two gay teenagers. In Iran, as well as a number of other countries, being homosexual is punishable by death.

ity and acceptance. This community's struggles, moreover, vary dramatically around the world. In many regions it is considered shameful to identify as LGBT. Over a third of countries worldwide still view homosexual acts as criminally punishable offenses, and in some countries—including Iran, Saudi Arabia, and Sudan—being homosexual is not only illegal, it is punishable by death.

In the United States pockets of opposition remain as well. Organizations and individuals that oppose LGBT rights are typically religious or socially conservative. Although some in this demographic

The Spread of LGBT Rights

Public attitudes toward LGBT rights have changed dramatically over the past several decades. The rise in support for same-sex marriage has been especially steep: According to Gallup polls, 60 percent of Americans support same-sex marriage today. This is up from just 27 percent when Americans were first polled in 1996. Meanwhile, Public Religion Research Institute surveys show that a majority of Americans oppose certain laws that discriminate against the LGBT community, such as bathroom bills that require transgender individuals to use bathrooms inconsistent with their gender identity.

Support for LGBT protections is not just an American phenomenon. The *Economist* describes how LGBT rights have swept the world:

> The leap forward has been startlingly quick. In the 1950s gay sex was illegal nearly everywhere. . . . Today gay sex is legal in at least 113 countries. Gay marriages or civil unions are recognized in three dozen and parts of others. In most of the West it is no longer socially acceptable to be homophobic. Gay life in China is now both legal and, in cities, undisguised. Latin America is even more gay-friendly. . . . Thais are more relaxed about transgender people than Westerners are. South Africa's constitution is remarkably pro-gay.

Economist, "The Gay Divide," October 9, 2014. www.economist.com.

are making great strides to accept the LGBT community and their rights, many of these same groups often oppose laws and policies that favor LGBT rights and well-being. For example, a poll by the Public Religion Research Institute in 2015 showed that 60 percent of Catholics and 62 percent of mainstream Protestants supported marriage equality. However, according to a report published just one year earlier, a majority of Americans believed gay sex is immoral. In fact, up to 14 percent believed that the AIDS virus is God's punishment for participating in homosexual behavior.

Furthermore, according to Mark Potok, senior fellow at the Southern Poverty Law Center, many people continue to view members of the LGBT community with suspicion and to use hateful terms like *faggot* to describe them. He says such comments and attitudes profoundly shape public perception of LGBT people. "They're described as perverts, as people who seduce children, as people who engage in horrible, unnatural practices," says Potok. "There's all kinds of hatred in this country, but it's rare to have a group described in such incredibly demeaning terms."[14]

Amid this anti-LGBT sentiment, US legislatures have introduced over 250 bills since 2013 that supporters fear will limit LGBT rights; 20 of these have been signed into law. In March 2016, for example, North Carolina signed House Bill 2 into law, which required all public facilities to permit people to use only bathrooms corresponding to the biological sex assigned at birth. The so-called bathroom bill sparked fierce national debate over the rights of transgender people. Although North Carolina's bill was repealed in March 2017, others like it enjoy widespread support.

Moreover, evangelical Christians and other groups continue to push for the passage of so-called religious freedom bills. These would give faith-based groups and individuals a religious exemption from providing services that are at odds with their religious faith, like catering or providing flowers for a same-sex wedding. A new bill in Kentucky would extend similar religious protections to students in public schools and universities. Many worry that the bill, if passed, would allow religious student groups and other groups to prohibit LGBT students from joining certain organizations solely on the basis of their sexual orientation or gender identity. Sarah Warbelow, legal director of the Human Rights Campaign, is among those who believe the Kentucky law is discriminatory. She states that school groups should welcome all students, or as she calls them, "all-comers." As Warbelow puts it, "When you do away with 'all-comers,' you send a message that LGBTQ students aren't welcome to participate in the full scope of the educational experience."[15]

> "There's all kinds of hatred in this country, but it's rare to have a group described in such incredibly demeaning terms [as are LGBT people]."[14]
>
> —Mark Potok, senior fellow at the Southern Poverty Law Center

Furthermore, a number of individuals and politicians remain staunchly opposed to same-sex marriage. A good example of why comes from former Republican National Committee chair Ed Gillespie, who is Catholic. Gillespie believes that people should not be forced to accept behaviors they find immoral, and he resents being made to feel bad for those beliefs. "I am happy to accept people for who they are and love them," he says. "I am tired, however, of being told that unless I am willing to support government sanction of same-sex marriage then I am guilty of bigotry, tired of having my religious convictions scorned instead of respected, tired of having my children being confronted with shocking images every time they turn on the television or go on the Internet."[16] Gillespie represents many Americans who are tolerant of the LGBT lifestyle but stop short of supporting full civil rights for these individuals.

Whether the LGBT community will retain its marriage rights or experience diminished civil rights under the administration of President Donald Trump is not yet known. For now, many LGBT advocates believe that only a profound shift in cultural attitudes will lead to lasting change. Numerous polls continue to show that LGBT people tend to fare poorly socially and economically compared to the heterosexual population, illustrating there is still much work to be done.

Criminalization

Focus Questions

1. How do US sodomy laws, although invalidated by a Supreme Court ruling in 2003, continue to impact the LGBT community?
2. Do you think that sovereign nations should have the right to incarcerate or otherwise punish adults for homosexual sexual activity? Why or why not?
3. Why are LGBT youth more likely to be arrested and thrown in jail than their straight peers?

In many parts of the world, various LGBT behaviors are considered criminal—and punishable—offenses. Many of the laws and policies that target this community focus on the prohibition of certain sexual acts.

Laws Against Homosexuality

Laws that prohibit homosexual activity have existed throughout human history. These statutes, often called sodomy laws, outlaw a variety of sexual acts deemed "unnatural" or "immoral." Although the prohibited acts might take place between homosexual or heterosexual couples, the laws usually target people who are detained or prosecuted solely because of their homosexuality.

During the first half of the twentieth century, there were both federal and state laws against sodomy in every state of America. These laws provided the legal basis for police officials and others to target LGBT people, organizations, and events. By the 1990s, however, societal forces were shifting public perception about whether the state could regulate consensual sexual activity. This shift was due in part to the gay rights movement, which was well under way by this time. A number of individuals, including those in politics, business, and the entertainment industry, started living openly—and proudly—as lesbians, gays, and bisexuals. With so many people coming out, the moral disapproval of homosexuality was slowly replaced with more tolerant views. As Lillian Faderman writes in *The Gay Revolution: The Story of the Struggle*, "More and more families and friends began standing up for gays and lesbians who were coming out to them; and even if some Americans knew no lesbian or gay people personally, they met them weekly in their own living rooms through endearing TV characters such as Ellen DeGeneres's 'Ellen,' and 'Will Truman' of *Will and Grace*. Things were clearly changing."[17]

In turn, many people started to view sodomy laws as a blatant invasion of privacy. In response to these new societal attitudes,

John Lawrence (right) and Tyron Garner (left), celebrate their 2003 Supreme Court victory in Lawrence v. Texas. *The ruling determined it was unconstitutional to prohibit sexual activity between consenting adults.*

many states moved to repeal these laws. By 2002 most sodomy laws in the United States had been overturned. The following year the Supreme Court ruled in *Lawrence v. Texas* that it was unconstitutional to prohibit sexual activity between consenting adults. This landmark decision invalidated the country's remaining sodomy laws.

Despite this, a handful of states—including Alabama, Florida, Idaho, Kansas, Louisiana, Michigan, Mississippi, Montana, North and South Carolina, Oklahoma, Texas, Utah, and Virginia—still have sodomy laws, although they were invalidated by the *Lawrence* decision and cannot be enforced. Nevertheless, human rights advocates argue that these laws damaged perception of the LGBT community and have contributed to the widespread discrimination and violence that affects this population today.

Furthermore, rights advocates assert that many LGBT Americans continue to feel the effects of these laws. Michigan, for example, is one of the states that still has sodomy laws, despite the fact that they are unconstitutional. Some of these laws specifically target homosexual behaviors. For example, some law enforcement officials use the state's "abominable and detestable crimes against nature" and "gross indecency" laws to harass and detain those who participate in homosexual activities. "LGBT people in Michigan continue to be charged with crimes . . . in which they let another person know they are interested in private, unpaid sex with another adult," says Rudy Serra, chair of the Executive Clemency Advisory Council for the state of Michigan. "LGBT people are still at risk of spending 15 years in state prison for acts that are perfectly legal in most other states."[18] Even if judges ultimately rule these laws unconstitutional, the legal battles to fight them are often costly—and humiliating.

Another example of how LGBT people are targeted is an incident that occurred in Louisiana, one of the states that retains its sodomy laws. In a public park in Baton Rouge in 2013, an undercover sheriff's deputy met another man and invited him to his home. Upon consenting, the man was arrested, although he had not engaged in any illegal activity. The arrest was part of a series of efforts to prohibit gay men from hooking up in public places. Rights advocates charge that these policies criminalize gay men for activity that would go unnoticed were it to occur between opposite-sex couples. While the state's sodomy laws do not directly legislate LGBT behaviors, the Louisiana example shows how the existence of these antiquated mandates indirectly puts lesbians, gays, bisexuals, and transgender people at increased risk for arrest.

Criminalization Around the World

As of 2017 the vast majority of developed countries had either repealed or amended antihomosexual laws. Today more than 120 UN member states carry no legal penalties for consensual, private sexual activity. However, there are many countries in which a person's sexual orientation or gender identity can result in arrest, imprisonment, torture, or death.

According to a 2015 report by the World Economic Forum, close to 3 billion people live in countries in which identifying as LGBT is considered a criminal offense. Of the more than seventy states or provinces that make same-sex sexual activity illegal, over thirty are in Africa, including Algeria, Ethiopia, Kenya, Morocco, and Zambia. Many of the statutes are particularly harsh. In Tanzania same-sex sexual activity is met with prison sentences of up to thirty years. In Uganda those convicted can be sentenced to life imprisonment. Nigeria, meanwhile, has the Same Sex Marriage Prohibition Bill, which not only prohibits marriage between homosexuals but also imposes a fourteen-year prison sentence on anyone who operates or takes part in gay clubs or organizations. "Because of this law the police treat LGBT people in any way that they please," said one LGBT supporter in Abuja, Nigeria. "They torture, force people to confess and when they hear about a gathering of men, they just head over to make arrests."[19]

> "They torture, force people to confess and when they hear about a gathering of men, they just head over to make arrests."[19]
>
> —An LGBT supporter in Abuja, Nigeria

Many Middle Eastern countries—such as Iran, Kuwait, Oman, Pakistan, Yemen, and others—also have laws that penalize the LGBT community. Reports from Saudi Arabia, for example, indicate that police regularly flog, beat, and imprison those accused of soliciting homosexual activity. In other areas in which homosexuality remains against the law, many who are convicted spend years in prison. The pun-

Assault in a Federal Prison

Members of the LGBT community are incarcerated at higher rates than the general public, and once in jail, they face an increased risk of violence and sexual assault. A transgender woman who served time on a drug charge recalls how prison guards failed to protect her from sexual abuse:

> I was put in blatantly dangerous housing situations where officials knew I would be taken advantage of. When I went to tell the prison staff that the guy that I was in the cell with had [assaulted me] when I tried to sleep, I was told that if I reported the assault the only place he could house me was in the SHU, which is isolation. I knew that being housed in the SHU would prevent me from participating in the drug program that was allowing me to qualify for early release and I would not be able to attend school programs that I was involved in.
>
> I chose to keep quiet about what was happening to me so that I could be part of the program and be released from prison 18 months early. No one should have to make the choice between enduring a longer prison sentence or being sexually assaulted.

Quoted in Zack Ford, "5 Stories of LGBT People Being Unfairly Treated by the Criminal Justice System," *ThinkProgress* (blog), May 7, 2014. https://thinkprogress.org.

ishment for homosexuality in Bahrain, for example, is a ten-year sentence. Once imprisoned, moreover, the condemned are often subjected to extreme maltreatment and abuse.

Many of the laws that prohibit same-sex behaviors are also used to detain or arrest transgender individuals, even though gender identity is not directly linked to sexual orientation. Although few laws specifically criminalize transgender people, arrests of individuals charged with cross-dressing have been reported in Kuwait, Nigeria, Saudi Arabia, and the United Arab Emirates, according to Human Rights Watch. In Malaysia sharia law (moral codes that govern religious life) prohibits a man from dressing as a woman and, in some areas, a woman from dressing as a man. Those who break this law are subject to fines and imprisonment.

According to a 2016 report by the ILGA, in more than ten countries, same-sex behaviors may even be punishable by death. These include Afghanistan, Iran, Mauritania, Nigeria, Pakistan, Qatar, Saudi Arabia, Somalia, Sudan, the United Arab Emirates, and Yemen. Some, like Mauritania, Afghanistan, and the United Arab Emirates, have laws that mandate the death penalty for homosexual activity, although reports are unclear as to whether any executions have actually occurred in these countries. However, in other places, death sentences have been carried out after a person is convicted of engaging in homosexual acts. The execution method is often brutal; in 2002, for example, the Saudi government put three gay men to death by beheading them.

However, just because a country does not specifically have laws that prohibit homosexual activity or target LGBT populations does not mean these individuals are safe. For example, even though Iraq has no countrywide law that expressly forbids homosexual behaviors, some areas have adopted sharia law to impose the death penalty for same-sex relations. In these places executions of LGBT individuals are commonly reported. As a 2015 ILGA report confirmed, "Iraq, although [the death penalty is] not in the civil code, clearly has judges and militias throughout the country that issue the death sentence for same-sex sexual behaviors."[20]

In other areas controlled by the Islamic State of Iraq and Syria (ISIS), judges condemn homosexual men to particularly grisly executions. In May 2016 in Syria, for example, ISIS officials charged a young man with the crime of same-sex sexual activity. In front of hundreds of bystanders, the man was reportedly blindfolded, handcuffed, and thrown to his death from the roof of a high-rise building. The deaths are sometimes videotaped as a warning to others. According to Khalid Abdel-Hadi, who publishes the only LGBT magazine in the Middle East, *My.Kali*: "Day after day, we read about how the Islamic State, militias and extremists handle the LGBT community in countries like Syria, Iraq, Yemen and Morocco. . . . [We often see] videos of LGBT individuals being thrown from tall buildings, head first, and then stoned by bystanders."[21]

"[We often see] videos of LGBT individuals being thrown from tall buildings, head first, and then stoned by bystanders."[21]

—Khalid Abdel-Hadi, publisher of the only LGBT magazine in the Middle East, *My.Kali*

Egypt is another country that does not have specific laws against same-sex sexual activity. Nevertheless, the LGBT community there is effectively criminalized, and law enforcement officials administer harsh punishments to those arrested or de-

A homosexual man receives eighty-two lashes with a cane at a sharia court in Banda Aceh, Indonesia. Many countries have laws that severely punish homosexual behavior.

tained on homosexuality-related charges. Although the country has made some strides in recognizing LGBT human rights, the ILGA calls the country "one of the most hostile states to LGBT people on the planet."[22] One reason is because Egyptian police reportedly arrest gay men and subject them to painful anal examinations. This supposedly helps the police determine whether the men have engaged in sexual intercourse with other men, a punishable offense.

> "Forced anal exams are invasive, intrusive, and profoundly humiliating, and clearly violate governments' human rights obligations."[23]
>
> —Neela Ghoshal, a senior researcher at Human Rights Watch

Although the UN Committee Against Torture declared that these tests have no scientific justification, their use persists. These forcible exams have been reported in at least five countries since 2011, despite widespread condemnation. As Neela Ghoshal, a senior researcher at Human Rights Watch, says, "Forced anal exams are invasive, intrusive, and profoundly humiliating, and clearly violate governments' human rights obligations."[23] A Tunisian student who was forced to endure such an exam in 2015 said the experience was completely degrading. "I felt like I was an animal. I felt I wasn't human," he said. "When I got dressed, they put handcuffs on me and I went out, feeling completely in shock. I couldn't absorb what was going on."[24]

The Consequences of Criminalization

In addition to violating people's rights, criminalization has other consequences that affect the LGBT community and wider society. For example, the fact that homosexuality is illegal in many countries has far-reaching public health consequences.

Knowing that homosexual activity is illegal makes people reluctant to get tested for sexually transmitted diseases. According to data from the World Health Organization and the United Nations Programme on HIV/AIDS, "Criminalization . . . has a dire effect . . . on efforts to prevent the spread of HIV. It can, for example, deter some of those most at risk of infection from coming forward for testing and treatment out of fear of being deemed a criminal."[25] Testing is critical to ensure that HIV-infected people are diagnosed early and receive treatment, which prevents the transmission of new infections.

Other countries' criminalization of homosexuality causes these countries to fail to take public health measures that could significantly improve life for many citizens. Consider Tanzania, in which nearly 30 percent of gay men are HIV positive. Despite these high infection rates, the country announced in 2016 that it would stop accepting financial aid from the United States to counteract the country's, and the entire continent's, HIV/AIDS epidemic. Backed by $65 billion in funding, this successful program helped Tanzania's infection rates drop from 12 percent in 2002 to 5 percent in 2016. During the same time period, the number of people receiving treatment rose from nearly 209,000 to over 700,000. Human rights advocates charge that denying medical treatment to a community that so desperately needs it is abusive and will likely increase the death toll from AIDS.

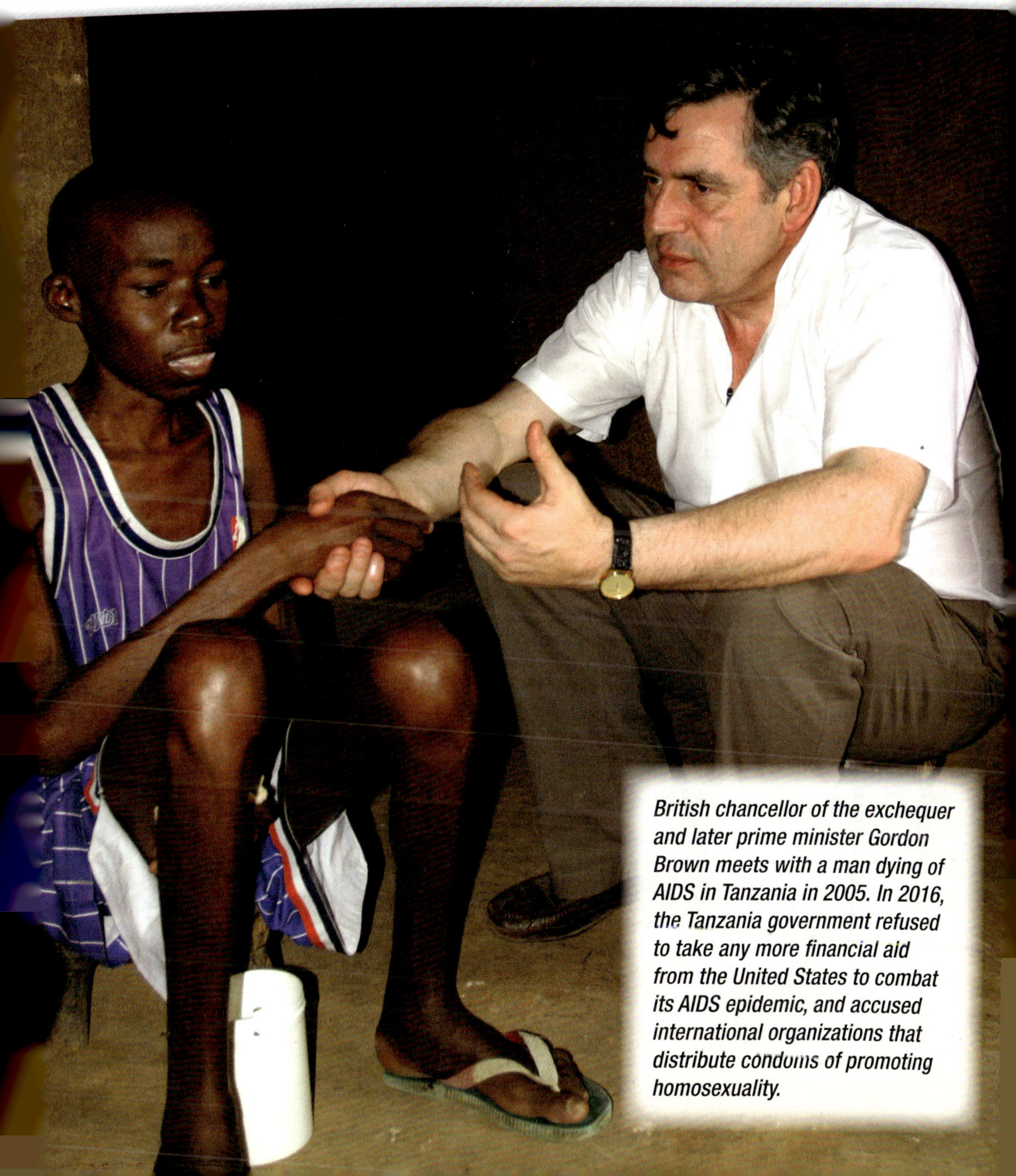

British chancellor of the exchequer and later prime minister Gordon Brown meets with a man dying of AIDS in Tanzania in 2005. In 2016, the Tanzania government refused to take any more financial aid from the United States to combat its AIDS epidemic, and accused international organizations that distribute condoms of promoting homosexuality.

Elected officials in Tanzania did not mince words while rationalizing their actions. The deputy minister of health, Hamisi Kigwangalla, accused international health care organizations that distribute condoms and teach people how to properly use them of "promoting homosexuality."[26] As one twenty-two-year-old Tanzanian man said, "It is clear that the government doesn't care whether we live or die."[27]

LGBT Overrepresented in the Criminal Justice System

In addition to criminal penal codes that directly violate people's basic human rights, there is another way that LGBT individuals enter the criminal justice system: through the enforcement of laws

Sodomy Laws Violate the Right to Privacy

American sodomy laws were overturned in 2003 in the landmark case *Lawrence v. Texas*. The case began in 1998, when John Lawrence and Tyron Garner were arrested after police found them in Lawrence's apartment engaging in homosexual activity. The two were charged with violating the state's "homosexual conduct" law. Lawrence appealed, asserting that the law was unconstitutional and violated the couple's right to privacy. Justice Anthony Kennedy wrote the majority opinion of of the Supreme Court in the case. In the ruling, Kennedy declared that sodomy laws violate Americans' constitutional right to privacy:

> [*Lawrence v. Texas*] does not involve minors. It does not involve persons who might be injured or coerced or who are situated in relationships where consent might not easily be refused. It does not involve whether the government must give formal recognition to any relationship that homosexual persons seek to enter. The case does involve two adults who, with full and mutual consent from each other, engaged in sexual practices common to a homosexual lifestyle. The petitioners are entitled to respect for their private lives. The State cannot demean their existence or control their destiny by making their private sexual conduct a crime. Their right to liberty under the Due Process Clause gives them the full right to engage in their conduct without intervention of the government. . . . The Texas statute furthers no legitimate state interest which can justify its intrusion into the personal and private life of the individual.

Anthony Kennedy, majority opinion, *Lawrence v. Texas*, June 26, 2003. www.law.cornell.edu.

that target LGBT individuals and communities. Indeed, members of the LGBT community have a disproportionately higher risk of being arrested and incarcerated compared to their heterosexual counterparts. Studies show that while gay and transgender youth make up only about 5 percent of the nation's youth population, they represent 13 percent to 15 percent of those in the juvenile justice system. This number may actually be low, as it is likely that there are more LGBT youth in the penal system who have not made their sexual orientation public. The rates are similar in adult populations: Roughly 16 percent of LGBT adults spend time in prison, compared to only 5 percent for the average American adult.

> "Out of despair and a need for survival, homeless gay and transgender youth are more likely to resort to criminal behaviors, such as drug sales, theft, or 'survival sex.'"[29]
>
> —Center for American Progress

One reason why so many LGBT youth become caught in the justice system is that this demographic is twice as likely to face family conflict, child abuse, or homelessness compared to other youth. A report by the Center for American Progress attributes this trend in part "to the fact that youth today 'come out' at younger ages, often to families that may not accept gay and transgender people. Since these youth still depend on their families to meet their material needs, family rejection can leave them emotionally and physically vulnerable, particularly if they find themselves cast onto the streets with nowhere to turn for support."[28]

Being homeless can set off a chain of events that leads to involvement in the juvenile justice system. "Out of despair and a need for survival, homeless gay and transgender youth are more likely to resort to criminal behaviors, such as drug sales, theft, or 'survival sex,' which put them at risk of arrest and detainment," according to the report. It goes on to say, "These youth are also at an increased risk of detainment for committing crimes related to homelessness, such as violating youth curfew laws and sleeping in public spaces."[29]

LGBT adults face similar obstacles. Discrimination in employment, housing, and other areas often make life difficult for LGBT individuals, who may not be able to find work, secure shelter, and meet other basic needs. Together, these factors increase the risk that LGBT adults will find themselves homeless and, like LGBT youth, be forced into illegal activities to support themselves. This in turn makes them likely to encounter police officials who promptly usher them into the criminal justice system.

Once in the system, LGBT people are often subject to bias and unfair treatment, according to many LGBT advocates. For instance, the justice system is often ill-equipped to understand the complex needs of LGBT teenagers and adults. Transgender individuals, for example, may be placed in facilities that do not conform to their gender identity. Punitive measures such as solitary confinement are unevenly applied to LGBT detainees, with reports indicating that 28 percent of LGBT youth are typically placed in solitary confinement, compared to only 18 percent of straight inmates.

Studies also find that LGBT prisoners are subjected to frequent sexual assault. Nearly 24 percent of transgender people in prisons reported being sexually assaulted by other inmates, while only 2 percent of heterosexual inmates were subject to such trauma, according to Human Rights Watch. LGBT inmates frequently report, moreover, that their pleas for help go unanswered.

Furthermore, the criminal justice system is often a point of no return for members of the LGBT community. Many face additional hardships once they are released from prison, because not only do they frequently face discrimination related to their sexual orientation or gender identity when searching for a new job or housing, they also have a criminal record, which hinders their chances of being able to earn a living. Therefore, LGBT individuals may suffer from the effects of punishment long after their sentence concludes.

As LGBT people steadily gain rights around the globe, they continue to remain overrepresented in the criminal justice system. Because their lifestyle and behaviors make them subject to arrest, incarceration, and other punishments in many parts of the world, rights advocates assert that the need for progress remains.

Discrimination

Focus Questions

1. Do you think business owners have a right to deny services to LGBT individuals if they think doing so would violate their religious principles? Why or why not?
2. Do you think that a person's sexual orientation or gender identity should be factored into a hiring decision? Explain your answer.
3. How do laws that require students to use restrooms that don't match their gender identity affect transgender individuals? How might they affect heterosexual individuals?

Despite legal progress and changes in public perception, those who identify as LGBT continue to face discrimination in work, employment, and many other areas of public life. According to a report by the global research group WORLD Policy Analysis Center, only five countries—the United Kingdom, Bolivia, Ecuador, Fiji, and Malta—grant full constitutional protections to their citizens regardless of sexual orientation or gender identity. A handful of other countries—including Mexico, New Zealand, Portugal, South Africa, and Sweden—give equal rights protections to people based on sexual orientation but not gender identity. Many LGBT advocates worry that the lack of constitutional protections leaves millions of people around the globe vulnerable to widespread discrimination and abuse.

The Challenge of Marriage Equality

Today more than forty countries legally recognize same-sex relationships. In the United States the 2015 ruling to legalize same-sex marriage evoked great optimism among LGBT advocates. In addition to ensuring the right to love whom one chooses, marriage equality confers a broad array of other rights. According to the Human Rights Campaign, there are more than one thousand legal rights associated with marriage, including access to health care, the right to receive Social Security benefits, and the right to file joint tax returns. Despite these positive changes, same-sex couples may still face challenges securing full recognition as a family. Chief among these challenges is the right for same-sex couples to raise a child together.

Even though adoption rights were a hallmark of the 2015 *Obergefell v. Hodges* decision, adoption equality has not been fully recognized. Part of the reason is that the adoption process in the United States is so complex that marriage equality alone is not enough to fully secure those rights. It is particularly challenging for LGBT couples to adopt a child that is not biologically theirs. Prospective parents may face discrimination if the social worker or adoption agency handling the adoption is biased against them. April Dinwoodie, chief executive of the Donaldson Adoption Institute, describes how these biases may prevent

Same-sex couples still face challenges securing full recognition as a family. Among these challenges is the right for same-sex couples to raise a child together and be legally recognized parents.

LGBT couples from becoming parents: "It's easy to find a way to say no to a couple. It's easy to prioritize some couples over others." If agents overseeing adoptions are prejudiced against LGBT adoption, "they can find something within a home study that doesn't suit them or find a reason a child wouldn't be a good fit for a home."[30]

Some states, moreover, have introduced policies that prevent same-sex couples from adopting children. For example, Michigan law allows Christian adoption agencies to deny services to LGBT parents seeking to adopt a child. At issue is the child's welfare. Those who are against LGBT adoption claim that children develop best when raised in traditional families. Many point to a widely cited study published in February 2015 in the *British Journal of Education, Society & Behavioural Sciences*, which reported that children raised by same-sex parents have more emotional problems than children raised by opposite-sex parents.

Supporters of LGBT adoption, on the other hand, counter that this study contained glaring methodological flaws and argue that children do not fare worse when raised by same-sex parents. As the pro-LGBT rights group Gay and Lesbian Alliance Against Defamation (GLAAD) says, "Studies have consistently shown that parenting by same-sex parents has no adverse effects on children."[31] In addition, many child welfare organizations, including the Child Welfare League of America and the American Academy of Pediatrics, have stated that someone's sexual orientation has no bearing on whether the person parents effectively. For now, policies and laws related to adoption and custody vary from state to state and will likely remain the subject of contentious debate.

Employment Discrimination

Some LGBT advocates have noted that achieving marriage equality may have created an unintended backlash that actually *increased* the risk of workplace and other forms of discrimination. Russell Roybal, deputy executive director of the National LGBTQ Task Force, describes what happened when many LGBT people rushed to marry following the *Obergefell* decision: "In a lot of places, you can go to your county clerk and get a marriage license and get married and then get fired the next week because now you are openly gay."[32]

Many LGBT rights organizations, including the Human Rights Campaign, report that employment discrimination remains a real problem within the LGBT community. In the United States there is no federal law that explicitly prohibits workplace discrimination against LGBT employees, save for a ban that prohibits discrimination against federal workers.

> "In a lot of places, you can go to your county clerk and get a marriage license and get married and then get fired the next week because now you are openly gay."[32]
>
> —Russel Roybal, deputy executive director of the National LGBTQ Task Force

According to the Center for American Progress, America's workforce includes close to 5.5 million LGBT individuals. Numerous studies report that discrimination against these workers is common. For example, a 2015 study published in the *Notre Dame Journal of Law, Ethics & Public Policy* found that up to 17 percent of lesbian, gay, and bisexual workers have been denied employment or fired on the basis of their sexual orientation. It also reported that up to 19 percent have been unfairly compensated in terms of salary, and up to 41 percent have been harassed by coworkers or bosses.

Discrimination against transgender employees is even more staggering: Forty-seven percent have been denied employment or fired, while nearly 80 percent have been harassed—either verbally or physically—by coworkers. According to the National Center for Transgender Equality and the National Gay and Lesbian Task Force, this group has rates of unemployment that are double the national average. One transgender woman named Vandy Beth Glenn was fired from her job as an editor and proofreader of legislative bills in Georgia when her boss found out she was transitioning from male to female. "My skills hadn't changed, my work ethic hadn't changed," says Glenn. "Because of [my gender change], the legislature I'd worked so hard for no longer had any use for my skills."[33] Because of their difficulty maintaining stable incomes, transgender individuals are perhaps the most economically vulnerable among LGBT people.

The Economic Cost of LGBT Discrimination

Some studies show that businesses that discriminate against their LGBT employees lose millions of dollars in lost productivity. According to an analysis by the World Bank in 2015, for example, India could be losing upward of $32 billion a year in economic output as a result of anti-LGBT discrimination. This waste of human potential impacts economies around the globe.

Conversely, a 2012 report by the Center for American Progress states that the top fifty Fortune 500 companies that have policies that prohibit discrimination against LGBT workers say that these policies have directly resulted in greater employee productivity and better morale. According to the report:

> Recruiting talented gay and transgender employees, retaining those employees, and ensuring they are performing at optimal levels enhances profitability and diminished unnecessary costs associated with employment discrimination. These . . . factors provide companies with strong financial incentives to cultivate a welcoming and inclusive culture for their gay and transgender employees.

Crosby Burns, "The Costly Business of Discrimination," Center for American Progress, March 2012. www.americanprogress.org.

Tackling discrimination sometimes becomes more complex when religious organizations are involved. Consider the case of Kristen Ostendorf, a former English and religion teacher at a Catholic high school. As per school policy, Ostendorf had signed an employment document stipulating that she could be fired from her job if she defied the teachings of the Catholic Church. Indeed, Ostendorf was let go after she announced she was a lesbian. Because of religious freedom laws, Ostendorf's dismissal was legal. As Catherine Conway, a lawyer specializing in employment law, says, "Freedom of religion is protected by the Constitution. . . . You can't tell a religious group—even if you disagree with it—to change its beliefs."[34]

As LGBT groups and individuals fight to secure more rights in the workplace, others contend that numerous provisions already exist that adequately protect LGBT employees. Though they vary by jurisdiction, many state, city, and local laws offer some protection against employee discrimination. In addition, Title VII of the Civil Rights Act of 1964, which prohibits discrimination based on gender, ethnicity, or religion, also includes discrimination against LGBT employees, even if such protection is not explicit. “These protections apply regardless of any contrary state or local laws,” states the US Equal Employment Opportunity Commission (EEOC). “Existing sex discrimination provisions in Title VII protect lesbian, gay, bisexual, and transgender (LGBT) applicants and employees against employment bias.”[35]

However, many LGBT supporters charge that there is no substitute for federal legislation that unequivocally protects LGBT workers. These advocates contend that Title VII is inadequate, for example, because it lacks specificity and is therefore open to interpretation. Federal courts, moreover, can reject the EEOC’s interpretation of existing laws. At the same time, close to thirty states lack laws that explicitly protect LGBT workers from losing their job due to their sexual orientation or gender identity.

LGBT Discrimination in Schools

For many individuals, anti-LGBT discrimination starts long before they enter the workforce. Indeed, LGBT students are often subjected to harassment, intimidation, and discrimination during

Parents protest at a school where a gay student was bullied and later committed suicide. School can be a hostile environment for students who identify as LGBT, prompting many officials to rethink their efforts against bullying.

their school years. According to a 2016 report by Human Rights Watch, many American schools are hostile environments for students who identify as LGBT. The report documented a host of discriminatory practices that leave many LGBT students feeling excluded and unsupported by school officials.

For example, Human Rights Watch reports that same-sex couples are sometimes prohibited from attending dances or other events as a couple. Student athletes contend that they have been barred from joining sports teams, while other students report that they are not allowed to talk about LGBT issues at school or that school administrators have discouraged them from forming a gay-straight alliance. They also describe extensive bullying and verbal slurs that go unpunished by school officials. "I've traveled around the country speaking to hundreds of LGBT students," says Ryan Thoreson, a fellow at Human Rights Watch. "They told me about feeling alienated, invisible, and unsafe in school."[36]

> "I skipped classes. I quit every extracurricular. I stopped participating in sports, gym and drama—anything that separated us by gender."[38]
>
> —A transgender high school student

The emotional effects of such harassment and discrimination—and the lack of reliable support from teachers and administrators—make learning difficult for many LGBT students. As one transgender individual said, "If you put me in a place where I am terrified, I'm not going to learn."[37] Another transgender student said that the bullying she endured in high school was so bad that she avoided school altogether to escape her tormentors. "I skipped classes. I quit every extracurricular. I stopped participating in sports, gym and drama—anything that separated us by gender."[38] A 2015 report by the Gay, Lesbian & Straight Education Network (GLSEN) indicates that experiences like these are not unique. The network found that LGBT middle and high school students experience pervasive harassment and intimidation and are more likely to skip school and have lower grades and less likely to graduate than heterosexual or gender-conforming students.

Human rights advocates contend that school administrators must do more to tackle the sometimes discriminatory school environments that interfere with LGBTs students' right to an education. "The Constitution guarantees all students, including LGBT students, access to safe and equal education," says Emily Greytak, GLSEN director of research. "But right now, LGBT students across the country are deprived of equal learning."[39] How far support for LGBT students should extend, however, remains a subject of debate.

The Public Restroom Controversy

Debate also surrounds transgender students' access to bathrooms, locker rooms, and other facilities. In August 2016 the US government stated that schools should allow students to use bathrooms that do not match their birth sex. These federal guidelines stated that prohibiting students from doing so is a form of sex discrimination that is banned under Title IX, an amendment to the Civil Rights Act that prohibits sex discrimination in federally funded schools. Opponents, however, argued that states and local governments should be left to deal with these issues on their own. US secretary of education Betsy DeVos was one such opponent. She claimed that this is an issue best left to schools, communities, and families, which "can find—and in many cases have found—solutions that protect all students."[40] DeVos and others made their case successfully, and in February 2017 the US Department of Education and the US Department of Justice revoked the guidelines that protected transgender students.

LGBT advocates lamented that accommodations for transgender students had been removed. Many worry about students like a fourteen-year-old transgender girl in Texas, who said she was assaulted by a group of football players after she was forced to use the boys' locker room. "I had to strip down into my girly underwear in front of a bunch of guys who would call me these rude names,"[41] she says. Opponents of policies that prohibit students from using bathrooms, locker rooms, and other facilities that match their gender identity believe that schools are putting the health and safety of transgender students at risk.

On the other hand, many balk at the idea that a student should be allowed to use a restroom with members of the opposite sex. Vicki Wilson is the mother of a student who attends high school in Palatine, Illinois. There school officials allowed a transgender girl to change in the girls' locker room. Wilson says that while she feels sympathy for students working out their gender identity

People protest North Carolina's HB2 law, a law that restricted the use of public bathrooms by transgender people. While the law was repealed in 2017, other states have filed similar bills.

issues, she believes that "young men shouldn't be permitted to deal with those issues in an intimate setting like a locker room with young women. . . . No school should impose a policy like this against the will of so many parents."[42]

Without a federal directive, schools will likely look to their state governments as they decide to what extent transgender students are made vulnerable by current policies. To this end, a number of lawsuits are currently working their way through the courts. These so-called bathroom battles extend far beyond public schools, however. Many are popping up across the country. Although the

Marriage Equality: Opposition Remains

Many groups and individuals opposed the Supreme Court's 2015 ruling to uphold marriage equality for LGBT couples. One such opponent was Kentucky county clerk Kimberly Davis, who immediately garnered national attention when she refused to issue marriage licenses to same-sex couples. When a federal court gave her a specific order to issue the licenses or risk losing her job, Davis dug in further, citing her religious faith as a reason to withhold the marriage licenses. She continued to describe her fear that she would go to hell for violating a central teaching of the Bible. Support for Davis from opponents of same-sex marriage was quick to follow, notably from former Arkansas governor Mike Huckabee.

Supporters of the court's ruling were quick to point out the hypocrisy of Davis's stance, as she herself had been caught committing adultery (another forbidden act in the Bible), had been married to four different men, and had given birth to children fathered by other men while still legally married to another. Consequentially, LGBT supporters argue that the Davis example illustrates why public opinion must be addressed before full marriage equality is achieved.

most publicized bathroom bill, in North Carolina, was repealed in 2017, other states, including Alabama, Missouri, South Carolina, and Washington, have filed similar bills.

Other Accommodations and Services

Battles are also raging over what kind of access LGBT individuals should have to other public establishments and services, including retail, entertainment, and other community places. At issue is whether private businesses and employees should be forced to provide goods and services if doing so would violate their moral convictions or religious beliefs. For example, some people assert that providing services for a same-sex wedding runs counter to the religious stance held by some that marriage is strictly between a man and a woman. To reflect these views, the First Amendment Defense Act was introduced in 2015. If enacted, the bill would prohibit the federal government from penalizing businesses that decide not to provide services to LGBT individuals on the basis of these types of moral and religious beliefs. LGBT rights supporters fervently oppose the act. Emily Martin, vice president of Workplace Justice at the National Women's Law Center, calls the bill "a license to discriminate," adding that "religion can be used to justify a lot of ugly things."[43]

A flurry of bills similar to the First Amendment Defense Act have been debated at the state level. In April 2016, for example, Mississippi enacted a law that allows businesses to refuse service to individuals if doing so would violate the business owner's or employees' religious beliefs or moral convictions. Many believe that business owners should have a right to refuse service to those whose lifestyle offends what they believe to be moral. It is from this position that many individuals are taking a stand against what they call government intrusion.

One such person is Barronelle Stutzman, a Christian florist in Washington State who refuses to sell flower arrangements to couples having same-sex weddings. The state's Supreme Court ruled that Stutzman was in violation of antidiscrimination statutes, but Stutzman argued that forcing her to commercially participate in an event she regarded as morally wrong was actually a violation of *her* rights. Stutzman was so grounded in her belief that she vowed to take her case to the US Supreme Court. "It was terrifying when you think that the government is coming in and telling you what to think and what to do and what to say,"[44] she comments.

> "It's wrong for the state to force any citizen to support a particular view about marriage or anything else against their will."[45]
>
> —Kristen Waggoner, Alliance Defending Freedom attorney

Groups like the Alliance Defending Freedom work to protect what they call religious freedom and thus support business owners like Stutzman who refuse to comply with anti-discrimination laws. "In a free America, people with differing beliefs must have room to coexist," says Alliance Defending Freedom attorney Kristen Waggoner, who argued in support of Stutzman's right to refuse service to the couple. "It's wrong for the state to force any citizen to support a particular view about marriage or anything else against their will. Freedom of speech and religion aren't subject to the whim of a majority; they are constitutional guarantees."[45]

Like so many issues related to LGBT causes, these religious freedom laws and others that have been proposed or enacted across the country draw intense scrutiny and debate. Human rights advocates and other LGBT allies believe that tackling these discriminatory laws and policies is essential if LGBT individuals are to be fully protected members of society.

Chapter 4

Violence and Harassment

Focus Questions

1. Do you think that the Hate Crimes Prevention Act adequately protects the LGBT community against hate crimes and violence? Why or why not?
2. What do you think motivates the disproportionate levels of violence directed toward the LGBT community?
3. What effect do you think verbal slurs and other forms of bullying have on LGBT youth, specifically?

Long before the rampage against LGBT club goers at the Pulse nightclub in 2016, LGBT people were frequent targets of violence and hate. While the scope of human suffering on that night captured the world's attention, most of the violence against LGBT individuals is not as visible or large scale. Rather, it occurs at the individual level—in homes, schools, and on the streets. According to Melissa Batchelor Warnke, contributing columnist for the *Los Angeles Times*:

> The Orlando attack gave many straight people a glimpse into what LGBT Americans have known all along: that the world is dangerous if you're queer, more dangerous if you're also an ethnic or racial or religious minority. The victims went to Pulse nightclub to be themselves in what they thought was a safe corner of a hateful world. The price they paid was their lives. The Orlando attack chillingly underscores that, for LGBT Americans, there are no safe corners.[46]

The Importance of Matthew Shepard

Many LGBT human rights activists believe that the modern landscape of the LGBT community cannot be understood without including the story of individuals like Matthew Shepard, whose gruesome murder in 1998 set off a nationwide debate about anti-gay hate crimes—and led to legislation to counter them.

On October 6, 1998, a few months before Shepard's twenty-second birthday, he went to a local pub in Laramie, Wyoming, where he encountered two young men who, because Shepard

Two young men stand in court on charges of kidnapping and murdering college student Matthew Shepard in 1998. Shepard, who was gay, was severely beaten by the men and left in a remote area in near-freezing temperatures. He died six days later.

> "The Orlando attack gave many straight people a glimpse into what LGBT Americans have known all along: that the world is dangerous if you're queer."[46]
>
> —Melissa Batchelor Warnke, contributing columnist for the *Los Angeles Times*

was gay, lured him to a remote rural area, where they tied him to a fence. In a violent frenzy, the two beat and pistol-whipped Shepard and then left his unconscious body tied to the fence in near-freezing temperatures. When a bicyclist found him the next morning, his body was so battered and bruised that he was mistaken for a scarecrow. Shepard died six days later of his injuries.

The macabre story quickly gained national attention as people rushed to denounce Shepard's murder. Students at the University of Wyoming walked in their homecoming parade in silence in remembrance of him. Political leaders expressed deep sorrow over such senseless violence, and candlelight vigils were held all over Laramie. At the same time, activists around the country banded together to call for stronger legislation against hate crimes.

Up to that point, LGBT supporters had waged a losing battle to enact legislation that would specifically classify anti-LGBT violence as a hate crime. In the aftermath of the Shepard tragedy, new life was infused into the movement, now led by Shepard's parents, Dennis and Judy. Years of protests and rallies followed, and in 2009 then-president Barack Obama signed the Matthew Shepard and James Byrd Jr. (the latter a victim of a horrific race-based hate crime in Jasper, Texas, in 1998) Hate Crimes Prevention Act into law, adding sexual orientation and gender identity to the categories covered under federal hate crimes law.

This landmark bill built on protections against racially motivated hate crimes to include crimes against the LGBT community and those with disabilities. It also added multiple provisions to curtail hate crimes. First, a stipulation was removed that only protected hate crime victims who were targeted while participating in federally sanctioned events, such as voting or attending school. With the new legislation, perpetrators could be charged with hate crimes in any scenario. Second, the bill gave federal authorities the ability to investigate potential hate crimes that local law enforcement chose not to pursue. Lastly, it provided millions in funding for the investigation of hate crimes and required the FBI to begin keeping hate crime statistics on sexual orientation and gender identity, similarly to the way that other forms of hate crimes are monitored.

Aside from these federal protections, many states, but not all, have hate crime laws with specific protections for sexual orientation and gender identity. Some of these laws expand law enforcement resources and increase sentences in cases involving sexual orientation or gender identity.

These types of laws, however, are not without detractors. For example, many religious and conservative groups and individuals do not support hate crime legislation designed to protect the LGBT community on the grounds that such laws may erode religious liberty. In some cases individuals and groups cite the Bible as a moral foundation to justify the condemnation of homosexuality. Some opponents, for example, reference parts of Paul's Letter to

Hate Crime Laws Are Not Effective

Many individuals and groups that oppose hate crime laws do so because they do not believe that increasing prison sentences for those convicted of hate crimes will deter these types of crimes. LGBT advocates Michael Bronski, Ann Pellegrini, and Michael Amico argue that laws already exist that punish those who perpetrate crimes of hate against LGBT individuals. These advocates purport that anti-LGBT hatred and homophobia can only be solved by changing public attitudes, not mandating longer prison sentences:

> People who commit crimes and are caught usually get punished. Getting rid of hate crime laws would not let convicted criminals go free. The person who commits a second-degree felony in New York state can already go to prison for seven years. Is doubling—or, as the law euphemistically states it, "enhancing"—that prison sentence from seven to fifteen years going to make it more of a deterrent? . . . The place to change social attitudes, hearts, and minds is not in prisons. It is schools, in activist organizations, around the dinner table, at houses of worship, and other places where people can talk, disagree, and learn that disagreement may be a useful and even productive means of growth.

Michael Bronski, Ann Pellegrini, and Michael Amico, *"You Can Tell Just By Looking" and 20 Other Myths About LGBT Life and People*. Boston: Beacon, 2013, p. 167.

the Romans as proof of the inherent evil of homosexuality. Chapter 1, verse 32, for example, states that "God's justice requires that those who do these things [a list of sins which includes homosexual behaviors] deserve to die, yet they do them anyway."[47]

Vice President Mike Pence is among those who worry that hate crimes laws could be used to quell the right to express these types of biblical views. As a congressman lobbying against the Hate Crimes Prevention Act, Pence stated, "Individual pastors who may wish to preach out of Romans chapter 1 about what the Bible teaches about homosexual behavior . . . could be charged or subject to intimidation for simply expressing a biblical moral view on the issue."[48] While many in the LGBT community feel such

Vice President Mike Pence worries that hate crime laws could be used to interfere with the free-speech right to express opposition to homosexuality.

rhetoric places them in harm's way, Pence and those who agree with him fear the violation of the right the First Amendment grants them to express their moral opposition to homosexual behavior.

Additionally, little consensus exists regarding whether LGBT individuals are safer because of hate crimes statutes. For instance, some argue that hate crime bills do nothing to address the homophobic attitudes and other forces that lead to discrimination and violence in the first place. As Beverly Tillery, executive director of the New York City Anti-Violence Project, says, "There is still the feeling for some people that L.G.B.T. people are less than and don't matter, and that it is O.K. to commit acts of violence against them."[49] Statutes that lengthen prison sentences or mandate other harsher punishments for those who commit violence against LGBT people do nothing to address this mind-set. In fact, they may even result in offenders becoming more hardened, warn LGBT advocates. A better way to keep LGBT people safe, some believe, is to remove the stigma associated with being LGBT and to promote more sympathetic attitudes through educational and other programs.

A Pervasive Pattern of Violence

As the nation grapples with these legislative issues, crimes against this minority have continued. Today LGBT people are far more likely to be victimized by hate crimes than other minority groups. A 2014 report by the FBI found that close to 20 percent of all hate crimes reported targeted victims specifically because of their sexual orientation, and close to 2 percent of reported hate crimes involved victims being targeted because of their gender identity. The analysis also showed that LGBT individuals are more than twice as likely as African Americans to be the target of a violent hate crime. They are more than four times as likely as Muslims and almost fourteen times as likely as Latinos to be subjected to some form of violence or harassment.

According to the National Coalition of Anti-Violence Programs (NCAVP), homicides of LGBT people are on the rise. The coalition reported twenty-four documented murders of LGBT people in 2015, which reflects a 20 percent increase from 2014. "Every L.G.B.T person knows that our safety is not guaranteed," said a spokesperson for the group. "Although we don't live in fear and continue to be out and proud, it is still something that kicks around at the back of our head when we touch our partner's hand in public, when we lean in for a kiss, when we are out at a club being ourselves."[50]

Anti-LGBT violence affects transgender individuals disproportionately. Over one hundred transgender people were murdered worldwide in 2016, according to one study. In the United States at least thirteen such homicides are on record for the same year. While this number may not seem large at first glance, the transgender community constitutes a very small percentage of the overall population. These statistics suggest that transgender people are at increased risk of violent crime compared to other minority groups.

The NCAVP also reports that LGBT individuals who are also members of ethnic groups are more frequent victims of violence. According to the coalition, in 2015, 62 percent of all LGBT homicide victims were people of color, and 54 percent were transgender women of color. As one transgender woman remarked, "Killing us is nothing new. It's like being a policeman. When you go to work, you know you might get shot. It's just something that comes with the territory."[51]

> "Killing us is nothing new. It's like being a policeman. When you go to work, you know you might get shot. It's just something that comes with the territory."[51]
>
> —A transgender woman

Gregory Herek is a psychology professor at the University of California–Davis who studies antigay violence. He explains that the high rates of violence against the LGBT community may actually reflect a surge in support for LGBT individuals' basic right to security and dignity. As society becomes more tolerant and accepting, Herek contends, those who oppose LGBT rights may become more radical in their opposition. "They may feel that the way they see the world is threatened, which motivates them to strike out in some way, and for some people, that way could be in violent attacks,"[52] he says.

Making the issue more complicated is the fact that current statistics on the problem might not be accurate. Indeed, collecting data to quantify how many people are victimized by anti-LGBT attacks is another challenging issue. Many victims are afraid to report attacks or seek

Transgender Suicide

Dana Aliya Levinson is a transgender woman who advocates for LGBT rights. She describes how bullying and harassment led to thoughts of suicide that started when she was a young boy:

> When I was 10 years old, in the dead of night, I went down to the kitchen. I pulled a knife out of the drawer and placed it against my stomach. I tried to will myself to use it. I repeated this behavior for months, maybe even a year, on and off. . . .
>
> By the time I was that age, I knew that I "wanted to be a girl," and I knew that I was getting crushes on boys in my grade. I had been called a faggot everyday of my life from when I was in kindergarten through this moment, and beyond. . . .
>
> I was bullied, told I was inherently wrong, there was no space for me socially, and I couldn't see where I fit in the world. That's why I experienced such severe suicidal ideation [thoughts] at such a young age. That ideation came and went throughout my teenage years with peaks during puberty, which caused such intense psychological pain for me, and also during my early twenties in the few years preceding my transition. . . .
>
> I am grateful to my younger self that I didn't make such a rash and foolish decision. I have grown into a strong, proud and confident woman, and I have carved out space for myself in this world, bigotry be damned. I am grateful to be alive.

Dana Aliya Levinson, "Until the World Changes, My Transness Comes First," *Huffington Post*, February 23, 2017. www.huffingtonpost.com.

help because they fear being discriminated against at police stations and social services agencies and in the legal system. One transgender woman described what happened after a taxi driver drove his car into her after calling her a "freak" and "pervert. "I immediately reported [the attack to the police]. It was scary, no-one helped, [and] everyone was laughing."[53]

The 2014 FBI report found that for these and other reasons, many anti-LGBT crimes are never reported to police. Even those that are successfully reported may not be categorized as a hate crime based on sexual orientation or gender identity, due to the interpretation of police or other officials of what constitutes a hate crime against this minority. Thus, many who study these types of crimes believe the rates of violence and homicide perpetrated against the LGBT community are much higher than current statistics suggest.

Schools

Another place where violence and harassment is a problem is schools. By all accounts, bullying and harassment of LGBT students is particularly widespread. Many LGBT rights supporters contend, moreover, that most educational systems offer scant refuge for LGBT youth.

While students of all walks of life face social pressure at school, the experience can be far worse for LGBT students who lack reliable, confidential support. These students are far more likely than their heterosexual counterparts to be victims of verbal and physical abuse. According to studies in the United States, the United Kingdom, and Thailand, between one-half and two-thirds of LGBT students are regularly bullied at school; in response, many of these students ditch school or drop out altogether.

The first nationwide study in the United States yielded similar results. The study, administered by a division of the Centers for Disease Control and Prevention (CDC) in 2015, polled high schools students about their sexual orientation and frequency of violent encounters. As journalist Jan Hoffman reports, "These adolescents [lesbian, gay, and bisexual students] skipped school far more often [than straight students] because they did not feel safe; at least a third had been bullied on school property. And they were twice as likely as heterosexual students to have been threatened or injured with a weapon on school property."[54]

Transgender students report having particularly high levels of fear associated with school. According to the National Center for Transgender Equality, more than 75 percent of transgender students report being bullied and feeling unsafe at school. Said a seventeen-year-old transgender boy in Utah, "I've been shoved into lockers, and sometimes people will just push up on me to check if I have boobs."[55] When he talked to school officials about it, they blamed him for being open about his gender identity.

In some instances not only did teachers fail to provide protection, they themselves mocked homosexuality, traumatizing students even further. In fact, a report by the GLSEN found that 55 percent of LGBT students polled reported anti-LGBT discrimination by teachers, coaches, and other school personnel. For example, one seventeen-year-old bisexual female student described how her teacher made disparaging comments about homosexuality that made the student feel ashamed and humiliated. "My biology teacher my freshman year would bring in kids who were wearing short shorts or weird sweaters and say, "You'd better take that off, you're going to look gay.'"[56] Experiences like these increase the sense of shame and isolation these students feel and leave them not knowing where to turn for help. Says Ryan Thoreson of Human Rights Watch:

> "[LGBT students] not only have to deal with bullying by other students but also with faculty and staff who ignore bullying and harassment in the classroom, use anti-LGBT slurs, tell anti-LGBT jokes, or teach that being LGBT is wrong."[57]
>
> —Ryan Thoreson, Human Rights Watch

> Even as millennials generally become more supportive of their LGBT peers, many students I spoke with said they had been targeted for physical bullying, verbal harassment, sexual harassment, or cyberbullying. Worse, they not only have to deal with bullying by other students but also with faculty and staff who ignore bullying and harassment in the classroom, use anti-LGBT slurs, tell anti-LGBT jokes, or teach that being LGBT is wrong.[57]

At Risk for Mental Health Issues, Suicide, and More

With so many obstacles facing LGBT individuals, supporters contend it is not surprising that the LGBT community suffers from the variety of mental health issues it does. Numerous studies show that LGBT people, and especially youth, are far more likely to suffer depression and attempt suicide. Such experiences are often precipitated by bullying or other forms of harassment.

According to the CDC survey on adolescent sexuality, more than 40 percent of lesbian, gay, or bisexual students polled reported that they had considered suicide, and close to 30 percent had attempted to kill themselves in the year prior to taking the survey. By comparison, only 6 percent of heterosexual teens had attempted suicide during the same time period.

The story of Tyler Clementi, a gay student who committed suicide in 2010, painfully highlighted the intense personal suffering endured by many members of the LGBT community. Clementi, a freshman at Rutgers University, jumped to his death from a bridge after his roommate secretly recorded pictures of him kissing another man in his dorm room. Although Clementi's heartbreaking story made national news, his experience—showcasing how antigay harassment has tragic outcomes—is not unique.

Transgender youth are even more at risk. The 2015 study by the CDC reports that this group is ten times more likely to consider suicide, compared to gender-conforming youth. Many have experiences like Grace, a twenty-year-old transgender woman who says she was relentlessly bullied as a child. She recalls the

Jane Clementi looks at family pictures of her son Tyler. In 2010, Tyler, a gay student at Rutgers University, committed suicide after his roommate secretly recorded him kissing another man in his dorm room.

question she asked herself when she attempted suicide at age thirteen: "If I didn't belong, why should I be alive?"[58]

Although Grace survived, stories like hers are common among LGBT youth. LGBT supporters contend that legislation is needed to protect students who often endure rejection and ostracism in ways that feel unbearable to them. Although every state in the United States has enacted legislation aimed at curbing bullying in schools, as of 2016 only nineteen states and the District of Columbia specifically target bullying on the basis of gender identity and sexual orientation. California is among the states to take a strong stance against anti-LGBT bullying. There the legislature updated the state's antibullying laws to include sexual orientation and gender identity. Seth's Law, as the legislation is called, is named after a thirteen-year-old student who took his life in 2010 after enduring years of antigay bullying at school.

As untold stories of personal suffering continue to unfold across the country and around the world, many human rights supporters hope that more support for LGBT individuals is coming. Tragedies like the Pulse nightclub shooting, the murder of Matthew Shepard, and the suicide of Tyler Clementi illustrate how much work remains to create a safe environment for LGBT people.

Efforts to Protect the Human Rights of the LGBT Community

Focus Questions

1. Do you think federal legislation to protect against anti-LGBT discrimination is necessary? Why or why not?
2. What effect, if any, would teaching LGBT history as a part of mandatory school curriculum have on LGBT students? Explain your answer.
3. In what ways, if any, should businesses and corporate leaders participate in the fight for LGBT human rights? Explain.

While it is undeniable that a great deal of progress has been made, it would be premature to assume that the LGBT community has secured full human rights. There are, however, plenty of reasons for optimism about the future.

As a whole, society appears to be growing more accepting of the LGBT community. Human rights supporters attribute this to numerous factors, including an outpouring of empathy in the aftermath of tragedies like that in Orlando, widespread coverage of the anti-LGBT bullying epidemic, and a growing awareness that LGBT people are a vital part of society.

In addition, as society has become more tolerant, LGBT individuals have come out in greater numbers and at earlier ages, making it both hard for others to deny their existence and easier for families and communities to embrace them. As Kenneth Roth, the director of Human Rights Watch, puts it, “People suddenly discovered that they had a gay brother or son or neighbor or close colleague, which started shaping public perception and reinforced social change."[59]

Laws and Resolutions

Many LGBT activists fight for legislative and policy changes to reinforce the human rights of LGBT people. Currently in the United States, various state laws and Supreme Court rulings protect LGBT rights to some degree. However, there is no federal legislation that would unequivocally ban discrimination against the LGBT community. Activists would like to change that and thus supported those members of Congress who in 2017 introduced a bill that would amend the Civil Rights Act of 1964 to fully protect people based on gender identity and sexual orientation. As Roddy Flynn, executive director of the Congressional LGBT Equality Caucus, says of the

Young women participate in a gay pride parade. As society has become more tolerant, LGBT individuals have come out in greater numbers and at earlier ages.

> "People suddenly discovered that they had a gay brother or son or neighbor or close colleague, which started shaping public perception and reinforced social change."[59]
>
> —Kenneth Roth, director of Human Rights Watch

proposed Equality Act, "The power of having one document, one piece of legislation, that simply and clearly lays out the best path to legal equality cannot be overstated. If passed, all federal laws would be amended to explicitly ban discrimination against LGBT people."[60]

LGBT supporters contend that passing laws that publicly state that LGBT people are just as protected as heterosexual people would send the message that they are valued members of society. No longer would they be required by the government to keep their sexual orientation a secret, as they were in the military under the Don't Ask Don't Tell policy. No longer would businesses be allowed to discriminate against someone who is transgender. But perhaps most importantly, supporters think passing progressive laws would tell the rest of the world that the United States no longer condones bigotry as it pertains to sexual orientation or gender identity and is willing to take legal action to combat the discrimination and violence that has beset this group.

The LGBT community has gained some powerful allies around the world in its pursuit of rights. One is the UN. In September 2015, for example, then–UN secretary-general Ban Ki-moon delivered a plea for the protection of LGBT people around the world:

> In too many countries, lesbian, gay, bisexual, transgender and intersex people are among the poorest, most marginalized members of society. We need more data to get a clear picture—but we already know that gay affluence is largely a myth. Studies show that gay and lesbian people suffer disproportionate discrimination and abuse. They are rejected by their families . . . kicked out of their homes . . . and pushed out of school. Too many of our LGBT brothers and sisters are jobless, homeless and struggling to survive. . . . [We] understand that ending marginalization and exclusion of LGBT people is a human rights priority.[61]

The following year, the UN's Human Rights Council passed a resolution to protect LGBT people against discrimination and violence based on sexual orientation and gender identity and to appoint an independent expert to identify the causes of discrimination and violence. The resolution stated that all societies should be tolerant and respectful of the human rights of all people, including this vulnerable minority. LGBT activists and human rights activists more generally applauded this move. As Roth says about the resolution, "What happened at the UN is important as part of the effort to legitimize LGBT rights; to have such an overwhelmingly positive vote is an important rebuke to those governments that want to pretend homophobia and bigotry are consistent with international human rights standards. They're not."[62]

Other global efforts were spearheaded in Indonesia, where a group of LGBT experts developed a universal guide to apply international human rights law to abuses experienced by LGBT people. The guide, developed in 2006, is intended to facilitate the creation and application of human rights laws and policies throughout the world. Known as the *Yogyakarta Principles on the Application of International Human Rights Law in Relation to Sexual Orientation and Gender Identity*, the doctrine condemns

UN secretary-general Ban Ki-moon (center) speaks about the rights of LGBT people at a UN meeting in 2016. The LGBT community has gained support from the United Nations in its pursuit of rights and awareness.

dehumanizing practices that permeate less progressive nations, such as execution by the state, denial of employment, loss of custody of children, and any other degrading treatment or infliction of torture.

The Power of Role Models

Many of these desired changes for the LGBT community are already under way. Some attribute this to the growing proliferation of positive role models that show that LGBT people are like everyone else and have contributed to society in many ways. A study from the University of California–Davis found that the more lesbians, gays, and bisexuals a heterosexual knows, the fewer negative beliefs he or she holds about homosexuality. Watching television shows with gay characters was also found to have a positive impact on views about LGBT issues. Today media outlets are including a vast array of LGBT individuals, and this community is more visible than ever in films, movies, theaters, and literature.

Perhaps no other celebrity has had such a monumental influence on LGBT rights as Ellen DeGeneres. A soft-spoken, nonthreatening tomboyish actress, DeGeneres is best known for her talk show that has been on the air since 2003. She became famous for her role as "Ellen" on the comedic sitcom *Ellen* on

Softening Attitudes

The Catholic Church has historically opposed same-sex marriage, but many LGBT observers note that a paradigm shift may be occurring. In 2013 Pope Francis made waves among the global Catholic community when he declared, "If someone is gay and he searches for the Lord and has good will, who am I to judge?" This sentiment has traditionally been extremely unpopular among religious conservatives, so when the head of the Catholic Church and the dominant voice of Catholicism changed course on these views, the world community took note.

Pope Francis stopped short of endorsing marriage equality, citing the church's stance that a marriage is biblically defined as a union between a man and a woman. However, his tolerant views toward LGBT behaviors suggest that LGBT acceptance is on the rise.

Quoted in Rachel Donadio, "On Gay Priests, Pope Francis Asks, 'Who Am I to Judge?,'" *New York Times*, July 29, 2013. www.nytimes.com.

Perhaps no other celebrity has had such a monumental influence on LGBT rights as Ellen DeGeneres. The soft-spoken and nonthreatening actress is best known for her popular afternoon talk show.

ABC. DeGeneres, a lesbian, did not reveal her sexuality during the early years of her career. In 1997 the network took a calculated risk, and Ellen—the actress and the character—revealed herself as a lesbian on the show. DeGeneres was the first high-profile female celebrity to publicly acknowledge her homosexuality. The coming-out episode became a sensation, winning an Emmy Award and receiving enormous praise from LGBT supporters. Although multiple corporations pulled advertisements from the show in response to the anti-LGBT backlash, the overwhelming response was positive.

DeGeneres's courage opened the door for other public personalities to come out. For example, Jason Collins, a professional basketball player in the early 2000s, became the first active male athlete in any of America's Big Four professional sports leagues—Major League Baseball, the National Football League, the National Hockey League, and the National Basketball Association—to publicly express his homosexuality. In an interview with *Sports Illustrated*, Collins says, "I didn't set out to be the first openly gay athlete playing in a major American team sport. But since I am, I'm happy to start the conversation. I wish I wasn't the kid in the classroom raising his hand and saying, 'I'm different.' If I had my way, someone else would have already done this. Nobody has, which is why I'm raising my hand."[63] Other notable athletes to come out include Brittney Griner, a Women's National Basketball Association superstar for the Phoenix Mercury, and Michael Sam, a draftee of the then St. Louis Rams and the first NFL player to publicly reveal his sexual orientation.

LGBT individuals are also becoming more visible in public office. In November 2016, for example, Kate Brown, an open lesbian, was sworn into office as the governor of Oregon, making her the highest-ranking elected LGBT official in the United States. LGBT advocates interpret a victory in a fair election as a strong indication that the majority of citizens do not perceive homosexuality as a damning flaw or an undesirable quality. With Brown's victory paving the way, it is likely that other LGBT elected officials will follow in her footsteps.

Including LGBT Issues in School Curricula

Some argue that moving past negative stereotypes requires broader educational efforts in the nation's schools. LGBT advocates contend that teaching a curriculum that includes LGBT history and issues will lead to a more tolerant and inclusive society. Historically, LGBT topics have been barred from the classroom. To date, eight states, including Alabama, Arizona, and Texas, have laws that restrict schools from including LGBT topics as part of their curriculum or in-class discussions.

Many LGBT students say that these so-called no promo homo laws single them out for discriminatory treatment. One LGBT student in Pennsylvania recalls, "I remember in middle school, asking about same-sex relationships, and being totally shut down, and being pulled aside by an administrator and told that's not something we talk about."[64] According to Human Rights Watch, "These laws and policies [that prohibit teachers from addressing LGBT issues] send a strong signal to students that being LGBT is abnormal or wrong."[65]

This may be changing. In 2016 California became the first state to teach LGBT history in public schools, ensuring that future generations have a broader knowledge of LGBT history and a greater understanding of the many issues that affect this community. Under the Fair, Accurate, Inclusive and Respectful Education Act, signed into law in 2011 but not implemented until 2016 after much revision, the new curriculum adds "lesbian, gay, bisexual and transgender Americans . . . to the economic, political and social development of California and the United States of America, with particular emphasis on portraying the role of these groups in contemporary society."[66]

Rick Zbur, executive director of Equality California, believes this change will address many problems that plague LGBT youth, including lower graduation rates and higher suicide rates compared to their heterosexual and gender-conforming peers. "An LGBT-inclusive curriculum helps create an environment where all students can thrive," says Zbur. "And by seeing themselves reflected in lessons and materials, students' experiences are validated and their sense of self-worth validated, creating the opportunity for students to be able to achieve academically."[67]

> "This anti-family sexual engineering demonstrates how government-controlled schools have replaced academics with political correctness."[68]
>
> —Randy Thomasson, president of SaveCalifornia.com

Like many of the laws and policies related to LGBT issues, California's new policy is not without opponents. Conservative groups who do not support the curriculum charge that discussions about sexual orientation and gender identity are best left to parents and family. As Randy Thomasson, president of the pro-family group SaveCalifornia.com, says, "This anti-family sexual engineering demonstrates how government-controlled schools have replaced academics with political correctness."[68]

Help from Businesses and the Private Sector

As these changes in the nation's schools play out, the private sector is doing its part to push forward laws that favor the rights of LGBT individuals. Some businesses are choosing to make the work environment safer and more inclusive for LGBT employees. Others are in a unique position to push antidiscrimination policies far beyond the workplace.

Some global corporate organizations are using their advertising dollars and extensive reach to demand respect for the LGBT community. In 2016, for example, Kellogg's, a breakfast cereal company that has a long history of standing up for LGBT rights, announced it would stop advertising on Breitbart, a controversial news site that has featured homophobic, sexist, and racist news stories. Says Kellogg's in a news statement, "We regularly work with our media-buying partners to ensure our ads do not appear on sites that aren't aligned with our values as a company. . . . We recently reviewed the list of sites where our ads can be placed and decided to discontinue advertising on Breitbart.com."[69] So far, over eight hundred companies have blacklisted Breitbart.

These business-led boycotts appear to be having an economic impact. By one estimate, the state of North Carolina lost close to $400 million when the chief executive officer (CEO) of Deutsche Bank, John Cryan, decided to postpone planned expansion after the state's bathroom laws went into effect. Said Cryan in 2016, "We take our commitment to building inclusive work environments seriously. . . . We're proud of our operations and employees in North Carolina and regret that as a result of this legislation we are unwilling to include the state in our US expansion plans for now."[70]

> "[North Carolina's bathroom bill] has discriminated against our people and it has caused great economic harm in many of our communities."[71]
>
> —North Carolina governor Roy Cooper

Other businesses made similar moves out of North Carolina. The National Collegiate Athletic Association even relocated the 2016–2017 championship events out of the state as a protest against the law. Largely in response to this strong corporate reaction, the state repealed its bathroom bill in March 2017. Governor Roy Cooper acknowledged the heavy pushback when he said,

A Former Principal Speaks Out

Peter DeWitt is a former elementary school principal who works with schools and education leaders to improve public education. He believes that a curriculum that includes LGBT issues is necessary to help LGBT students feel safe and included in the school environment. DeWitt explains:

> Imagine walking into school each day and not hearing any stories through books or curriculum that depict the life you are living? The common language heard is used by peers in a negative way, and most adults don't intervene to stop it. Imagine that you attend a public school, but the "public" discussion that is accepted hardly ever mentions things you can relate to?
>
> That's how many LGBT students feel.
>
> Now that the Supreme Court made their historic decision regarding gay marriage it's time for LGBT issues and curriculum to be spoken about in schools. . . .
>
> Most schools have students who either identify as LGBT or have parents who are gay. The curriculum should at least mirror the real lives of these students.

Peter DeWitt, "3 Reasons Why Schools Won't Offer LGBT Curriculum," *Finding Common Ground* (blog), *Education Week*, May 21, 2017. http://blogs.edweek.org.

"For over a year now, House Bill 2 has been a dark cloud hanging over our great state. It has stained our reputation. It has discriminated against our people and it has caused great economic harm in many of our communities."[71]

Outside of North Carolina, a number of other well-known companies, including Apple, Coca-Cola, and Walt Disney, threatened to curtail operations in Georgia if a bill was passed that would allow business to deny services to LGBT patrons on the basis of religious freedom. As Disney said, "Disney and Marvel are inclusive companies, and although we have had great experiences filming in Georgia, we will plan to take our business elsewhere should any legislation allowing discriminatory practices be signed into state law."[72] In response to the condemnation, Georgia governor Nathan Deal vetoed the so-called license to discriminate bill, highlighting the role business can play in promoting social change.

According to Kenneth Roth, there is another way that businesses could bolster the cause of LGBT rights—by encouraging their CEOs and other executives to come out as LGBT. "It's sad that many corporate leaders still feel that they have to live in the closet," says Roth. "The more that corporations can highlight the LGBT people among their leadership, the quicker these societal transformations will be encouraged."[73] Progress is being made, however, since more business leaders are coming out. Trevor Burgess was the first openly gay CEO of C1 Financial, a publicly traded bank in the United States. "It's only a matter of time before openly gay people, people like me who have been authentic their entire adult lives, rise through the [corporate] ranks," says Burgess. "We have great examples in basketball, soccer, football and many other walks of life and now the [New York Stock Exchange]!"[74]

Many LGBT rights supporters hope that these milestones will continue to contribute to a shift in cultural attitudes toward the LGBT lifestyle and the benefits of diversity. With momentum building, these advocates hope to build a world community that fully embraces LGBT rights under the legal protections of human rights in the years ahead.

Introduction: A Pervasive Pattern of Violence

1. Quoted in Laurel Raymond, "Obama on Massacre at Gay Club in Orlando: 'An Attack on Any American Is an Attack on All of Us,'" *ThinkProgress* (blog), June 12, 2016. https://thinkprogress.org.
2. Quoted in UN News Centre, "Citing 'Pervasive Abuse,' New UN Report Presents Recommendations on Protecting LGBT Rights," June 1, 2015.www.un.org.
3. Ban Ki-moon, "Message to Human Rights Council Meeting on Violence and Discrimination Based on Sexual Orientation or Gender Identity," United Nations, March 7, 2012. www.un.org.
4. United Nations, Universal Declaration of Human Rights, December 10, 1948. www.un.org.

Chapter 1: A Global Overview of LGBT Human Rights

5. Quoted in Kelly Huegel, *GLBTQ: The Survival Guide for Gay, Lesbian, Bisexual, Transgender, and Questioning Teens*. Minneapolis, MN: Free Spirit, 2013, pp.18–19.
6. Quoted in James Janega, "First Gay Rights Group in the US (1924)," *Chicago Tribune,* October 30, 2013. www.chicagotribune.com.
7. Quoted in Jack Drescher, "Out of DSM: Depathologizing Homosexuality," *Behavioral Sciences*, December 2015. www.ncbi.nlm.nih.gov.
8. Quoted in Merdies Hayes, "United Front: LGBT Community Takes On Latest Challenges to Secure Rights," *OurWeekly*, June 24, 2016. http://ourweekly.com.
9. Quoted in Will Kohler, "June 28th, 1969: The Real History of the Stonewall Riots," Back2Stonewall, June 25, 2016. www.back2stonewall.com.
10. American Psychological Association, *Sexual Orientation and Homosexuality*, 2008 www.apa.org.
11. Mary Malia, "Why Gay Pride Still Matters and Isn't Just About Parades and Parties," *Huffington Post*, June 15, 2016. www.huffingtonpost.com.

12. Anthony Kennedy, majority opinion of the court, *Obergefell v. Hodges*, June 26, 2015. www.supremecourt.gov.
13. Quoted in US Naval Institute, "Key Dates in U.S. Policy on Gay Men and Women in Military Service," 2017. www.usni.org.
14. Quoted in Alonzo Weston, "After Orlando, Maybe It's Time to Look in the Mirror." *St. Joseph (MO) News-Press*, June 15, 2016. www.newspressnow.com.
15. Quoted in Iman Smith, "What Kentucky's Religious Freedom Bill Could Mean for LGBTQ Students," *PBS NewsHour*, March 23, 2017. www.pbs.org.
16. Ed Gillespie, *Winning Right: Campaign Politics and Conservative Policies*. New York: Threshold Editions, 2007, p. 249.

Chapter 2: Criminalization

17. Lillian Faderman, *The Gay Revolution: The Story of the Struggle*. New York: Simon & Schuster, 2015, p. 546.
18. Quoted in Carlos Maza, "State Sodomy Laws Continue to Target LGBT Americans," Equality Matters, August 8, 2011. http://equalitymatters.org.
19. Quoted in Human Rights Watch, "'Tell Me Where I Can Be Safe': The Impact of Nigeria's Same Sex Marriage (Prohibition) Act," October 20, 2016. www.hrw.org.
20. Aengus Carroll, "State-Sponsored Homophobia: A World Survey of Sexual Orientation Laws: Criminalisation, Protection and Recognition," International Lesbian, Gay, Bisexual, Trans and Intersex Association, October 2016. http://ilga.org.
21. Quoted in Jacob Wirtschafter, "In Much of the Middle East, It's Getting More Dangerous to Be Gay," PRI, August 30, 2016. www.pri.org.
22. Carroll, "State-Sponsored Homophobia."
23. Quoted in Human Rights Watch, "Dignity Debased: Forced Anal Examinations in Homosexuality Prosecutions," July 12, 2016.www.hrw.org.
24. Quoted in Human Rights Watch, "Dignity Debased."
25. United Nations Free & Equal, "Fact Sheet: Criminalization," 2016. www.unfe.org.
26. Quoted in Kevin Sieff, "Tanzania Suspends U.S.-Funded AIDS Programs in a New Crackdown on Gays," *Washington Post*, November 23, 2016. www.washingtonpost.com.

27. Quoted in Sieff, "Tanzania Suspends U.S.-Funded AIDS Programs in a New Crackdown on Gays."
28. Jerome Hunt and Aisha Moodie-Mills, "The Unfair Criminalization of Gay and Transgender Youth: An Overview of the Experiences of LGBT Youth in the Juvenile Justice System," Center for American Progress, June 29, 2012. www.americanprogress.org.
29. Hunt and Moodie-Mills, "The Unfair Criminalization of Gay and Transgender Youth."

Chapter 3: Discrimination

30. Quoted in Rebecca Beitsch, "Despite Same-Sex Marriage Ruling, Gay Adoption Rights Uncertain in Some States," *Huffington Post*, August 19, 2015. www.huffingtonpost.com.
31. GLAAD, "Family Portraits." www.glaad.org.
32. Quoted in Liam Stack, "The Challenges That Remain for L.G.B.T. People After Marriage Ruling," *New York Times*, June 30, 2016. www.nytimes.com.
33. Quoted in Faderman, *The Gay Revolution*, p. 571.
34. Quoted in Jennifer Calfas, "Employment Discrimination: The Next Frontier for LGBT Community," *USA Today*, August 1, 2015. www.usatoday.com.
35. US Equal Employment Opportunity Commission, "What You Should Know About EEOC and the Enforcement Protections for LGBT Workers." www.eeoc.gov.
36. Ryan Thoreson, "Michigan's LGBT Guidelines Deserve an A," Human Rights Watch, May 16, 2016. www.hrw.org.
37. Quoted in Philippa H. Stewart, "Witness: A Teacher Unable to Protect LGBT Students," Human Rights Watch, December 7, 2016. www.hrw.org.
38. Quoted in Marissa Higgins, "LGBT Students Are Not Safe at School," *Atlantic*, October 18, 2016. www.theatlantic.com.
39. Quoted in Higgins, "LGBT Students Are Not Safe at School."
40. Betsy DeVos, "U.S. Secretary of Education Betsy DeVos Issues Statement on New Title IX Guidance," US Department of Education, February 22, 2017. www.ed.gov.
41. Quoted in Human Rights Watch, "United States: Transgender Students at Risk," September 14, 2016. www.hrw.org.

42. Quoted in Sandhya Somashekhar et al., "Trump Administration Rolls Back Protections for Transgender Students," *Washington Post*, February 22, 2017. www.washingtonpost.com.
43. Quoted in Alicia Adamczyk, "What's at Stake for LGBT Rights in the Workplace Under President Trump," *Time*, November 16, 2016. http://time.com.
44. Quoted in Dave Urbanski, "Christian Florist Who Refused to Make Gay Wedding Arrangements to Take Case to U.S. Supreme Court," Blaze, February 17, 2017. www.theblaze.com.
45. Quoted in Alliance Defending Freedom, "Washington Floral Artist to Ask US Supreme Court to Protect Her Freedom," February 16, 2017. www.adfmedia.org.

Chapter 4: Violence and Harassment

46. Melissa Batchelor Warnke, "LGBT Americans Have Always Lived Under the Threat of Violence. Will Orlando Force Straight People to Acknowledge It?," *Los Angeles Times*, June 15, 2016. www.latimes.com.
47. Romans 1:32, New International Version.
48. Quoted in Michael Bronski et al., *"You Can Tell Just by Looking" and 20 Other Myths About LGBT Life and People.* Boston: Beacon, 2013, p. 165.
49. Quoted in Stack, "The Challenges That Remain for L.G.B.T. People After Marriage Ruling."
50. Quoted in Liam Stack, "The Challenges That Remain for L.G.B.T. People After Marriage Ruling."
51. Quoted in Samantha Michaels, "It's Incredibly Scary to Be a Transgender Woman of Color Right Now," *Mother Jones*, June 26, 2015. www.motherjones.com.
52. Quoted in Haeyoun Park and Iaryna Mykhyalshyn, "L.G.B.T. People Are More Likely to Be Targets of Hate Crimes than Any Other Minority Group," *New York Times*, June 16, 2016. www.nytimes.com.
53. Quoted in Lee Broadstock, *Transphobic Hate Crime*, True Vision. http://report-it.org.uk.
54. Jan Hoffman, "Gay and Lesbian High School Students Report 'Heartbreaking' Levels of Violence," *New York Times,* August 11, 2016. www.nytimes.com.

55. Quoted in Human Rights Watch, "'Like Walking Through a Hailstorm': Discrimination Against LGBT Youth in US Schools," December 7, 2016. www.hrw.org.
56. Quoted in Regina Garcia Cano, "Report: LGBT Students Still Face Discrimination at School," Associated Press, December 7, 2016. https://apnews.com.
57. Ryan Thoreson, "Toxic Homophobia Still Festers in America's Schools," Human Rights Watch, December 16, 2016. www.hrw.org.
58. Quoted in Laura Ungar, "Transgender People Face Alarmingly High Risk of Suicide," *USA Today*, August 16, 2015. www.usatoday.com.

Chapter 5: Efforts to Protect the Human Rights of the LGBT Community

59. Kenneth Roth, "LGBT: Moving Toward Equality," World Economic Forum, 2015. http://reports.weforum.org.
60. Quoted in Zach Stafford, "After a Historic Year for LGBT Rights in US, 2016 May See Backlash and Complacency," *Guardian* (Manchester), December 30, 2015. www.theguardian.com.
61. Ban Ki-moon, "Secretary-General's Remarks at the High Level LGBT Core Group Event 'Leaving No-One Behind: Equality & Inclusion in the Post-2015 Development Agenda,'" United Nations, September 29, 2015. www.un.org.
62. Roth, "LGBT."
63. Quoted in Joe Sterling and Steve Almasy, "NBA's Jason Collins Comes Out as Gay," CNN, April 30, 2013. www.cnn.com.
64. Quoted in Human Rights Watch, "United States: LGBT Students Face Discrimination," December 7, 2016. www.hrw.org.
65. Human Rights Watch, "United States."
66. Quoted in Alex Grubbs, "California Soon to Be First State to Teach LGBT History in Public Schools," CNS News, July 20, 2016. www.cnsnews.com.
67. Quoted in Becca Andrews, "California Now Has an LGBT-Inclusive Curriculum," *Mother Jones*, July 19, 2016. www.motherjones.com.
68. Quoted in Grubbs, "California Soon to Be First State to Teach LGBT History in Public Schools."

69. Quoted in Dylan Byers, "Kellogg Pulls Ads from Breitbart," CNN Money, November 30, 2016. http://money.cnn.com.
70. Quoted in Stephanie Thomson, "These Businesses Are Boycotting Sexist, Racist Media," World Economic Forum, December 1, 2016. www.weforum.org.
71. Quoted in Jason Hanna, "North Carolina Repeals 'Bathroom Bill,'" CNN, March 30, 2017. www.cnn.com.
72. Quoted in Justin Carissimo, "Disney and Marvel Threaten to Boycott Filmmaking in Georgia over Anti-Gay Bill," *Independent* (London), March 23, 2016. www.independent.co.uk.
73. Roth, "LGBT."
74. Quoted in Emily Cohn, "Meet the First Openly Gay CEO of a Publicly Traded Bank," *Huffington Post*, August 28, 2014. www.huffingtonpost.com.

By getting involved, you can make a difference. Organizations that work with LGBT groups often need volunteers for a variety of tasks ranging from letter writing to organizing events. Some organizations also sponsor internships for youth.

American Civil Liberties Union (ACLU)

125 Broad St., 18th Floor
New York, NY 10004
www.aclu.org

The ACLU is one of the nation's oldest civil rights watchdog groups. Its mission is to defend the individual rights and liberties guaranteed by the Constitution and US laws. The ACLU has branches in each state that provide information on issues affecting young people, including LGBT rights and equal protection under the law. The branches also offer information on how to get involved with the organization.

Amnesty International (USA Headquarters)

5 Penn Plaza, 16th Floor
New York, NY 10001
www.amnestyusa.org

Amnesty International is a global organization focused on protecting human rights, with branches around the globe. The organization conducts research, disseminates information, and puts pressure on governments through lobbying and other activities both to prevent abuses of human rights and to demand justice when rights, including LGBT rights, have been violated.

GLSEN

1001 Connecticut Ave. NW #206
Washington, DC 20036
www.glsen.org

Devoted to change, GLSEN (pronounced "glisten"; formerly the Gay, Lesbian & Straight Education Network) works with students, schools, parents, and the community to ensure that students in the LGBT community are safe in their school environments. It provides training and support at the national and local levels for educators, principals, district leaders, and government leaders who work toward building school cultures that embrace the differences of their LGBT students.

GLAAD

5455 Wilshire Blvd. #1500
Los Angeles, CA 90036
www.glaad.org

Formerly the Gay and Lesbian Alliance Against Defamation, GLAAD advocates for LGBT rights and holds the media accountable for the image it presents to the public about the LGBT community. The group seeks to promote a true understanding of LGBT lives. By increasing awareness, GLAAD hopes to decrease the stigma, stereotyping, and marginalization of those within the LGBT community.

Human Rights Campaign (HRC)

1640 Rhode Island Ave. NW
Washington, DC 20036
www.hrc.org

The HRC is the largest LGBT civil rights advocacy organization in the United States, representing a force of more than 1.5 million members worldwide. The HRC operates at both a grassroots level and nationally. Its website offers a trove of information on LGBT legal rights at both the state and national level.

Human Rights Watch (HRW)

350 Fifth Ave., 34th Floor
New York, NY 10118
www.hrw.org

The HRW is a nonprofit organization that conducts research and publishes reports on human rights violations around the globe. In addition to drawing international attention to human rights abuses, including LGBT abuses, the HRW puts pressure on governments and international organizations to reform abusive practices. The organization provides internships in field offices throughout the world.

International Lesbian, Gay, Bisexual, Trans and Intersex Association (ILGA)

20 Rue Rothschild, 5th Floor
1202 Geneva, Switzerland
www.ilga.org

ILGA seeks to promote lesbian, gay, bisexual, transsexual, and intersex equality through the worldwide cooperation and mutual support of its members. It focuses public and government attention on cases of discrimination by supporting programs and protest actions, applying diplomatic pressure, and working with international organizations and the international media.

National LGBTQ Task Force

1325 Massachusetts Ave. NW, Suite 600
Washington, DC 20005
www.thetaskforce.org

The National LGBTQ Task Force works to build a future where everyone is free to be themselves in every aspect of their lives. The organization trains and mobilizes millions of activists throughout the nation to remove the barriers that lesbian, gay, bisexual, transsexual, and questioning people face in every aspect of their lives: in housing, employment, health care, retirement, and basic human rights.

Books

Ann Bausum, *Stonewall: Breaking Out in the Fight for Gay Rights*. New York: Speak, 2015.

Adrian Brooks, *The Right Side of History: 100 Years of LGBTQ Activism*. New York: Cleis, 2015.

Lillian Faderman, *The Gay Revolution: The Story of the Struggle*. New York: Simon & Schuster, 2015.

Cleve Jones, *When We Rise: My Life in the Movement*. New York: Hachette, 2016.

Kevin L. Nadal, *That's So Gay! Microaggressions and the Lesbian, Gay, Bisexual, and Transgender Community.* Washington, DC: American Psychological Association, 2013.

Nancy Orel and Christine Fruhauf, *The Lives of LGBT Older Adults: Understanding Challenges and Resilience*. Washington, DC: American Psychological Association, 2014.

Internet Sources

Anti-Defamation League, "ADL and the LGBT Community: A Commitment to Equal Rights," 2017. www.adl.org/education/resources/backgrounders/adl-lgbt-community-a-commitment-to-equal-rights.

GLAAD, *GLAAD Media Reference Guide*. 10th ed. New York: GLADD, 2016. www.glaad.org/sites/default/files/GLAAD-Media-Reference-Guide-Tenth-Edition.pdf.

Human Rights Watch, *Shut Out: Restrictions on Bathroom and Locker Room Access for Transgender Youth in US Schools*. New York: Human Rights Watch, 2016. www.hrw.org/sites/default/files/report_pdf/uslgbttrans0916_ web.pdf.

Movement Advancement Project and GLSEN, "Separation and Stigma: Transgender Youth & School Facilities," April 2017. http://lgbtmap.org/transgender-youth-school.

Pew Research Center, "A Survey of LGBT Americans," June 13, 2013. www.pewsocialtrends.org/2013/06/13/a-survey-of-lgbt-americans.

Mark Potok, "QUACKS: 'Conversion Therapists,' the Anti-LGBT Right, and the Demonization of Homosexuality," Southern Poverty Law Center, May 25, 2016. www.splcenter.org/20160525/quacks-conversion-therapists-anti-lgbt-right-and-demonization-homosexuality.

Kenneth Roth, "LGBT: Moving Towards Equality," World Economic Forum, January 23, 2015. www.hrw.org/news?news-type%5B%5D=9428.

Williams Institute, "Media Advisory: Fact Sheet on Guidance Protecting over 350,000 Transgender Youth and Young Adults from Discrimination," February 22, 2017. https://williamsinstitute.law.ucla.edu/research/transgender-issues/media-advisory-fact-sheet-on-guidance-protecting-over-350000-transgender-youth-and-young-adults-from-discrimination.

Note: Boldface page numbers indicate illustrations

Cover: iStock.com/Mattjeacock

5: John Panella/Shutterstock.com

9: Associated Press

12: Hallett Ron Mirrorpix/Newscom

15: DM1 WENN Photos/Newscom

20: Associated Press

25: Pacific Press/Sipa USA/Newscom

27: STR/Reuters/Newscom

32: Ramon Espelt Photography/Shutterstock.com

36: Associated Press

39: J. Bicking/Shutterstock.com

43: Associated Press

46: Evan El-Amin/Shutterstock.com

52: Associated Press

55: Shawn Goldberg/Shutterstock.com

57: Lucas Jackson/Reuters/Newscom

59: Featureflash Photo Agency/Shutterstock.com